*Dialogue: The Key
to Understanding
Other Religions*

*Biblical Perspectives on Current Issues*

HOWARD CLARK KEE, General Editor

# Dialogue: The Key to Understanding Other Religions

DONALD K. SWEARER

THE WESTMINSTER PRESS
PHILADELPHIA

PUBLISHED BY THE WESTMINSTER PRESS ®
PHILADELPHIA, PENNSYLVANIA

PRINTED IN THE UNITED STATES OF AMERICA

Library of Congress Cataloging in Publication Data

Swearer, Donald K   1934–
    Dialogue, the key to understanding other religions.

    (Biblical perspectives on current issues)
    Includes bibliographical references.
    1. Christianity and other religions. 2. Chris-
tianity and other religions—Buddhism. 3. Buddhism
—Relations—Christianity. I. Title. II. Series.
BR127.S93    261.2    77–3964
ISBN 0–664–24138–7

To Bikkhu Buddhadāsa
an inspiration
to interreligious dialogue

# Contents

*Editor's Preface,* by Howard Clark Kee      11

*Foreword,* by Douglas V. Steere      13

*Preface*      19

1   Approaches to Interreligious Dialogue      25
2   In the World But Not of It      51
3   It Is No Longer I Who Live      69
4   True Righteousness      84
5   Freedom Now!      100
6   A Kingdom of Priests and a Holy Nation      120
7   A Buddhist View of Christianity      136

*Notes*      169

# Editor's Preface

One powerful sign of the turning inward that has marked the retreat from the violence and activism of the late 1960's has been the surge of interest in Eastern spirituality. The evidence for this ranges from the tract-passing, shave-headed, pink-robed Hare Krishna zealots on Sproul Plaza in Berkeley to the learned dialogues at ecumenical gatherings of theologians from New York to New Delhi.

The open attitude toward understandings of the divine-human encounter other than those of the Western Christian tradition is to be admired and encouraged. Yet much of the response to Eastern religions has been merely instinctive and therefore non-reflective. Reaction to the rise of interest in these Oriental religions from within the church is bounded on one side by flat rejection of any approach to God that deviates from the evangelical tradition. On the other side there is a readiness to adopt any ideas or practices that will stimulate some kind of direct religious experience.

How should Christians approach other religions? This is a current issue that becomes increasingly urgent in the face of our growing awareness that we live in a global village. What posture can Christians assume toward others of a different religious tradition that requires neither the surrender of our own convictions nor the disparagement of the convictions of others? Out of concern that the church will address itself thoughtfully and responsibly to the challenge of the Eastern religions particularly, Donald K. Swearer was asked to prepare this book.

Intentionally, the assignment was specific. He was not to

attempt to correlate a sweeping view of Oriental spirituality with Christianity in general. Rather, as a kind of test case, he was asked to explore the relationship between one important facet of the Christian faith—in the letters of Paul—with a concrete and coherent type of Eastern faith—Theravāda Buddhism.

Having lived for extended periods of time in Thailand, where he was in frequent conversation with both Christian and Buddhist thinkers, Professor Swearer is well qualified to offer a firsthand account of the relationship of these faiths. As an unusually effective teacher—at Oberlin, and more recently at Swarthmore and Bryn Mawr—he is skilled in interpreting concepts and insights across cultural, religious, and academic lines.

It is wholly appropriate that, following Donald Swearer's exposition on his theme, there is a rejoinder from a Buddhist scholar, equally concerned for interreligious relationships, and already familiar with Professor Swearer's thought. Some readers will be critical of Buddhadāsa's restatement of the Christian faith. But the very fact that a thoughtful, sympathetic observer of Christianity responds to it in this way is itself an important revelation. It indicates how our faith appears to an outsider who stands within a cultural tradition other than our own. The book, therefore, both embodies dialogue and invites it. The author and his respondent, as well as the editor, will be gratified if the readers of this book are moved by it both to examine afresh the basis of their own faith and to seek ways in which the faith of another tradition can be perceived with empathy. Perhaps from such a thoughtful encounter understanding and respect can be extended and our own commitment and experience can be enriched.

HOWARD CLARK KEE

*Bryn Mawr College*

# Foreword

Donald Swearer, in this book, addresses the issue of how Christians approach other world religions. After exploring various positions that have been taken, he advocates dialogue as holding the most promise. He then proceeds to conduct such a dialogue between Thai Theravāda Buddhism and his own Christian experience and heritage. Throughout the book he is in territory that is still only sparsely explored and he is doing it conscious of the real stakes that are involved.

I have often recalled a vivid moment in the final Abraham Flexner Lecture in a series that Arnold Toynbee gave thirty years ago at Bryn Mawr College. He startled several academic historians who sat near me by declaring that a thousand years from now when the history of this twentieth century of ours comes to be written, the historians would be very little interested in the episode of the conflict between communism and the nations committed to a freer polity and economic system. What they would really want to know would be what happened to both Christianity and Buddhism when for the first time in history they interpenetrated each other! Donald Swearer is seeking in this book to describe some of the factors that will play a part in one small corner of that interpenetration. In the course of this description he draws attention to its immense importance for the psyches of both of these great religions. He also explores certain ways in which this penetration can be creative, and criticizes others that will close rather than open the doors to each other.

Plant breeders have discovered that exposing seeds to radiation produces fresh unpredictable mutations that with careful selection and nurture can produce improved varieties of plants. In something not unlike this, exposure, if intense enough, to another great world religion has often revealed neglected or hidden facets of immense importance in one's own religion. Somewhat in this fashion Donald Swearer uses the irradiating power of Theravāda Buddhism as he has experienced it in Thailand. After discussing the nature of creative dialogue in the opening chapter, he goes on in the chapters that follow to describe the fresh focus and insights which such exposures have released in regard to his own Western Christian tradition and experience. In this way he treats Buddhism's massive devaluation of the transitory; its systematic attempt to dissolve away the me-ness of the self; the dealing with the issue of faith and works; the rigorous use of meditation as an agency of freedom; and the amazing use of the widely spread net of monasteries as support groups to service the householders and build a solidarity between the monks and the people.

This approach has profound implications for the teaching of world religions. Some years ago, a meeting at Princeton Theological Seminary gathered a number of the country's most distinguished authorities in the field of the history of religions. Wilfred Cantwell Smith, at that time the head of the Center for the Study of World Religions at Harvard University, provoked a vigorous debate. He suggested that the same principles that had been fruitful in the personal dialogues between members of the great world religions be applied to the teaching of courses in this area. He affirmed that unless the leaders in the field of the history of religions were to remain content simply to imitate the past, some radical experimentation was called for. He reminded them that all the sacred texts in the field of the world religions had now been adequately translated and were readily available. There were ample institutes where the original languages in which these texts were written, Sanskrit, Pāli, Arabic, Hebrew, and the rest, could be mastered. In addition, they now had a rich outlay of sermons, folklore, and art that could enrich and illuminate these studies. All of this had been accomplished.

What was missing and what cried out for attention and experimentation were means to enable the student to come into a living dialogue with the religion that he was studying. To do this would require that the student meet and come to know persons for whom the religion he was studying was a transforming experience. He needed to learn how to bracket the hasty judgments that pour up from the religion and culture with which he is familiar. It was necessary that he learn to make an interior space in which he could begin to grasp what the world looked like when seen through the eyes of the faith he was confronting.

What Professor Smith did not say, but what seemed to be provokingly implicit in his suggestion, was that in this kind of approach there were serious risks that neither teacher nor student might find either congenial or compatible with the academic contract! In academic circles until now, there has been a sharp line drawn between gurus and scholars. The very citadel of academic objectivity might be threatened in such an undertaking.

The uneasiness and rigor of debate that these challenging suggestions aroused in the Princeton gathering would seem, however, to be authentic signals that Professor Smith had struck at the real nerve of the issue. For if we would really understand another religion, if we are interested in the central thrust that has created the world view in which an active adherent of that religion lives and makes his choices, in the practices that have opened this world view to him and renew him in it, we cannot avoid the existential realm. We cannot help being searched by it. There is no detour around the risk of having it irradiate our own cosmic orientation. It may even effect certain changes of stance in the religious and cultural posture in which we have been living.

It is very difficult to have this type of breakthrough experience without some personal contact with an active adherent of another religion who has enough scholarly bent to be able to communicate his insight and experience effectively. When such a breakthrough takes place it can become an invisible spectator of all that occurs in a student's consciousness. It becomes a kind of, let us say, Buddhist presence that is there querying, encouraging, broadening the spectrum in which the student's future experience of his own religion takes place.

When Jane Addams went out to speak about her Halsted Street settlement house in Chicago, she is said to have had a habit of taking along a woman who lived in that street and who knew what the settlement did and didn't do. She would ask the woman just to sit in the audience while she spoke in order to keep her closer to the truth. She seemed to feel that the silent presence of that woman at the meeting queried statements and enthusiasms that up to that time she had taken for granted. The woman's mere presence may even have exercised a real influence on what she actually said!

If this kind of experience of penetrating and being penetrated by the silent presence of a world religion that a person is studying is thought to be desirable, then a wide variety of experiments must be undertaken in the period that lies ahead to allow it to happen. To my own knowledge, there have been few more creative innovators in this area than Donald Swearer. In an earlier book, *Secrets of the Lotus,* he describes a four-week exposure of a group of his Oberlin College students to Buddhism. There was a fortnight of daily lectures and actual practice of the Theravāda form of Insight Meditation under a Thai Theravāda meditation master. This was followed by a similar period of Zen instruction and practice by a skilled Japanese Zen Buddhist monk. In his world religions courses at Swarthmore, where he is presently teaching, he has from time to time provided a kind of laboratory period each week where the students may have close touch with an articulate adherent of the religion that is being studied and where some practice of exercises that are its vehicle of renewal can be carried out.

This book is a record of further personal exploration that he has carried out and of further breaking of new ground. In this amazing century, there are literally no walls between the East and the West. A growing ecumenism has not only pierced barriers between the Christian churches but has roused the great world religions to make a few gestures toward learning how to be present to one another. They are seeking ways to begin to share their inward treasures with one another, and how to feel the beginnings of some sense of responsibility for one another and for the Himalayan needs of the world. In spite of all this we are still only at the very beginning. Perhaps in the whole undertaking of which this book is a symbol, the word of a contemporary is the best we can muster for our condition when he says: "Not in your strength or in your skill but in your need, shall you be blessed."

DOUGLAS V. STEERE

*Haverford College*

# Preface

In the spring of 1973, I was invited by the Thailand Theological Seminary to deliver the eighth series of the Sinclair Thompson Memorial Lectures. The series was established to promote better understanding between Christians and Buddhists in Thailand. It was named after a Presbyterian missionary who took interreligious understanding as one of the aims of his work, cut short by his untimely death in the early 1960's. I was honored to accept the invitation, both because of the purpose to which the lectures are dedicated and because of my personal acquaintance with Rev. and Mrs. Thompson and their daughter, a former student of mine at Swarthmore College.

This present volume, with the exception of the last chapter, has developed out of those lectures delivered to an audience of Buddhists and Christians in the Buddhist Association Assembly Hall, Chiang Mai, Thailand. The ideas were further refined in a series of lectures given at Pendle Hill in early 1976. The concluding chapter is composed of a selection from the seventh Thompson lecture series, presented by Bhikkhu Buddhadāsa, Thailand's foremost interpreter of Buddhism, and my response to it. I am grateful to Bhikkhu Buddhadāsa and the Thompson Lecture Committee of the Thailand Theological Seminary for permission to publish selections from his lecture series. I wish also to thank the Thailand Theological Seminary for granting me permission to revise my lectures and to publish them in the United States. I am particularly grateful to Bhikkhu Buddhadāsa and his publisher in Thailand, The Sublime Life Mission, for permission to edit and include his materials here.

In many respects this volume is a personal theological statement. I was brought up in the Presbyterian church and have seminary degrees, but for the past decade I have spent most of my time studying and teaching Buddhism and other Asian religions. Buddhism has strongly enticed me and I have felt deeply the truth of many of its claims. My study of Buddhism, therefore, has caused me to reconsider my Christian faith in a new light. Indeed, my involvement in the study and teaching of Buddhism has enlarged and deepened my own particular faith stance.

Another factor in my personal history has also influenced this volume. During the more than ten years I have taught undergraduates they have been asking serious questions about the validity of American society, a society that has been closely identified with institutional Christianity. Both implicit and explicit in their critique of American social, political, and economic institutions is a criticism of the religious institutions identified with them. Their ofttimes revolutionary suggestions for correcting social ills belie a deep undercurrent of frustration and uncertainty, anxiety and fear. Many students feel surrounded by unknowns, by forces beyond their power, depleting them and their environment of the opportunity of living humanely. In the midst of such an ethos these undergraduates are often searching for new levels of meaning and new modes of spirituality. Some find them in Buddhism. Most students of my acquaintance do not declare themselves to be Buddhists, but they find that their own quest for meaning can be enriched by their study of Asian religions.

The context for this volume, then, includes my own particular religious upbringing and study of both Western and non-Western religions. It also includes my appreciation of the relatively uncertain feelings that young people have about the future, and the relevance that Buddhist insights might have for them as they go about the process of assessing their own faith stance as Christians, Jews, or nontraditional religious persons.

In the light of this context, two or three comments about the nature of this book seem both obvious and appropriate. The title, DIALOGUE: THE KEY TO UNDERSTANDING OTHER RELIGIONS, indicates an open rather than an exclusivistic stance toward other faiths. There are Biblical passages that make exclusive claims for Christianity and eminent spokesmen for such a position. This book does not really argue the merits of two different Christian approaches to non-Christian religions. Rather, it tries to make a case for what we are calling a dialogical approach. Furthermore, we shall not discuss "other religions" in general, taking bits and pieces from a variety of non-Christian faiths. Rather, the focus is on the non-Christian tradition that I know best, namely, Theravāda Buddhism, the normative Buddhist tradition in Sri Lanka, Burma, Thailand, Cambodia, and Laos. Buddhist terms occur primarily in their Pāli form, the canonical language of Theravāda Buddhism, although familiar terms—e.g., Nirvāna, Tripiṭaka—appear in their Sanskrit form. The primary cultural referent will be Thai Buddhism. An analogous selection occurs in Christianity as well. In this volume I am taking a position fashioned largely in Pauline and Augustinian terms. By this I do not mean that I am trying to examine fully the thought of Paul and Augustine; rather, that I see justification for the general thrust of my position in insights found in their thought.

As I focus primarily on only one non-Western religious tradition, two presumptions are being made: (1) that we are limited in our ability to enter deeply into more than one religious tradition outside of our own, and (2) that the principles derived from an in-depth encounter between two religious traditions will be useful in other dialogical contexts. Limiting the scope of the dialogue serves to eliminate the problem of talking about religion in general, an entity that does not exist. Furthermore, it ensures more opportunity for

depth and breadth of study, not only of the normative teachings but also of the particular religions' cultural and institutional histories. Too often our knowledge of a religion, even
our own, is based on inadequate study and understanding.
Obviously, problems of this nature will be even greater with
traditions other than our own.

My own interest in interreligious dialogue developed
unexpectedly. I had spent several years in this country and
in Asia studying Buddhism in preparation for research and
teaching. I did not study Buddhism from a Christian perspective or with the intent of finding parallels between the two
traditions. On the contrary, following the canons of objective
scholarship, I did my best to bracket my own assumptions
and value judgments. My obligation as a scholar and a
teacher was to study Buddhism on its own terms, and to
communicate a sympathetic and critical understanding of its
truth claims. Only after several years, when invited to present the Thompson lectures, did I consciously engage in the
dialogical enterprise. Only then did I begin to ruminate how
my study of Buddhism had affected my own faith. Perhaps,
at its best, interreligious dialogue emerges from such situations, a natural encounter that develops almost as though by
accident (or providence!). To approach another religion with
a hidden agenda can produce only limited results, often
more negative than positive. To study Buddhism, for example, with the *intent* of comparing it with Christianity must
necessarily undermine the integrity of the Buddhist tradition
itself.

There are, of course, many levels on which dialogue can
be engaged. It can be carried on primarily within a particular
philosophical framework to which the languages of faith are
referred. For example, currently several Christian theologians and Zen philosophers are engaging in dialogue within
the philosophical framework of process philosophy. Another
level would be to examine the symbol systems of Christianity
and Buddhism to see if they engage common human prob-

lems—e.g., suffering, conflicting loyalties, moral virtue—in such a way that sympathetic comparison can lead to mutual enlightenment. This book proposes such a task through a comparison of the terms, concepts, and idioms that form the symbol systems of these two traditions. The dialogue attempts to be self-reflexive. That is, here is a dialogue in which a Christian contemplates Buddhist teachings, and then in the light of that study reflects on how his own faith has been challenged, enlarged, and deepened. The other side of the dialogue is represented in part by the last chapter. Here a Buddhist contemplates Christian teachings for what they can contribute to his own beliefs. The parallel, however, is not exact.

Many people in both Thailand and America have been helpful and encouraging in my initial plunge into interreligious dialogue. My wife, Nancy, has shared in the development of many of these ideas. Francis Seely, president of the Foundation for Inter-Religious Dialogue, deserves special mention for his efforts to promote a mutually beneficial encounter among Buddhists and Christians in Thailand. P. Linwood Urban, chairman of the Department of Religion at Swarthmore College, read the entire manuscript and offered invaluable suggestions throughout, as did Howard Clark Kee, the editor of this series. I wish to thank Anek Liang and the Thompson Lecture Committee of the Thailand Theological Seminary for the invitation to give the Thompson lectures in 1973, and Muak Chilangkarn for his translation of the lectures into Thai. My interest in doing this volume also owes a debt to John Cobb, School of Theology at Claremont, and Peter Hodgson, Vanderbilt Divinity School, who read and responded favorably to my Thompson lectures. Ruth E. Deer not only typed the manuscript with incredible efficiency but corrected grammatical and spelling errors. Finally, despite the help and encouragement I have received from others, I must claim responsibility for the inaccuracies, misguided notions, and faulty logic that might appear. It is my hope that there will be an opportunity for *dialogue* with those who disagree with the general posture of this book, for it is through dialogue that we grow in wisdom and understanding!

D.K.S

*Swarthmore College*

# Chapter 1

# Approaches to Interreligious Dialogue

Christian approaches to non-Christian religions evidence many faces. The purpose of this chapter will be to outline what some of these faces have been, first, from the perspectives of church history, second, from selected contemporary approaches, and, finally, from our own dialogical position.[1] The issue of Christianity and non-Christian religions is as old as the Christian community itself. It cannot easily be separated from the early church's understanding of the authority of its Lord and the nature of its relationship to him. E. C. Dewick argues that the message and character of Jesus as presented in the Gospels lead to the conclusion that a Christian attitude toward other religions should be "charitable and courageous, impartial and decisive. It will not encourage a thoughtless, good-natured acceptance of new ideas, without considering whether or not they are true, nor yet a wholesale condemnation of everything that does not bear the name or label of 'Christian.' "[2] Certainly, however, many New Testament passages indicate that the early followers made exclusive claims for Jesus: "All things have been delivered to me by my Father; and no one knows the Son except the Father, and no one knows the Father except the Son and any one to whom the Son chooses to reveal him" (Matt. 11:27); or, "No one comes to the Father, but by me" (John 14:6). An exclusivistic approach to non-Christian religions dominates both the Bible and the history of the church.

The roots of the exclusivistic claims of the Bible lie in the monotheism of the Old Testament which gradually developed over pre-Davidic, monarchical, and exilic times. The pre-Davidic period was henotheistic, the worship of Yahweh and Canaanite gods existing independently side by side. Yahweh was worshiped at the Canaanite shrines and the Israelites must also have worshiped the Canaanite agricultural deities. It is in this context that the writers of Exodus and Deuteronomy assert the supremacy of Yahweh over all other gods: "You shall have no other gods before me. You shall not make for yourself a graven image, or any likeness of anything that is in heaven above, or that is in the earth beneath, or that is in the water under the earth" (Ex. 20:3–4). And: "I am the LORD your God, who brought you out of the land of Egypt, out of the house of bondage. You shall have no other gods before me" (Deut. 5:6–7). Yahweh as the supreme God of the Israelites reigned supreme over Chemesh, god of the Moabites (Judg. 11:24), and the psalmist goes even further when he asserts that in relationship to Yahweh all other gods are but idols (Ps. 96:5).

Israelite religion during the monarchical and exilic periods becomes more strongly monotheistic, as Ps. 96 suggests. Ringgren observes in this regard that the concept of "sons of the Most High (*'elyōn*)" in Ps. 82 and "sons of God" (or "sons of gods") in Ps. 29 and 89 may represent a downgrading of Canaanite gods to the status of divine or heavenly beings.[3] They are likened to counselors or servants of the one king. Deutero-Isaiah signals the beginning of the radical monotheism with which most Christians associate Biblical religion: "I am the LORD, there is no other, besides me there is no God" (Isa. 45:5). And: "Turn to me and be saved, all the ends of the earth! For I am God, and there is no other" (Isa. 45:22). This writer, with whom we most often associate the suffering servant motif appropriated by the New Testament writers, was equally important in formulating exclusivistic claims later applied to Jesus. New Testament Christianity, therefore, is the inheritor of the theological viewpoint of exilic and post-exilic Judaism which had moved from a position where Yahweh was affirmed as the highest God among other gods to being the one and only God, the exclusive Lord not only of the Israelites but also of the universe.

The New Testament is filled with passages either directly or indirectly supporting an exclusivistic position toward competing truth claims. The writer of The Acts likens Jesus to a cornerstone without whom there can be no salvation: "There is salvation in no one else, for there is no other name under heaven given among men by which we must be saved" (Acts 4:12). The Epistles as well as the Gospels (see Matt. 11:27 and John 14:6) also affirm the exclusive and universal authority of Jesus. The conclusion to the famous Christological hymn of Philippians—"That at the name of Jesus every knee should bow, in heaven and on earth and under the earth, and every tongue confess that Jesus Christ is Lord, to the glory of God the Father" (Phil. 2:10–11)—is echoed in Ephesians. There Christ stands "far above all rule and authority and power and dominion, and above every name that is named, not only in this age but also in that which is to come" (Eph. 1:21). Both passages are reminiscent of Deutero-Isaiah. In short, there are strong Biblical grounds supporting a Christian position that would reject non-Christian religions as representing untruth. We cannot really know the precise theological content of the Great Commission—"Go therefore and make disciples of all nations, baptizing them in the name of the Father and of the Son and of the Holy Spirit, teaching them to observe all that I have commanded you; and lo, I am with you always, to the close of the age" (Matt. 28:19–20). However, as we shall see, the church has most often interpreted it to mean that outside of the gospel there is no salvation.

In the first three centuries the church was basically on the defensive against other religions as it sought to maintain itself against paganism. For the next twelve hundred years the church's policy toward non-Christian religions changed from defense to attack, and Christian intolerance became more unyielding than the previous attitude of the Roman Empire had been toward Christianity.[4] While the Protestant Reformation challenged the empirical institutional form of the one historic, holy, and catholic church, and deism and rationalism raised questions about whether Christianity is indeed the one and only true religion, "there was little disposition to recognize that the Divine Spirit was operating as a living power outside the Church."[5] In the nineteenth century the development of scientific and historical knowledge encouraged a tendency among liberal Christians to look more sympathetically at non-Christian religions. That same century, however, saw the rise of a great missionary movement. By the beginning of the twentieth century there were fifty thousand missionaries in all parts of the world who claimed some ten million converts to Christianity.[6]

From such broad historic trends E. C. Dewick outlines several attitudes that have come to characterize the church's posture toward other religions. They include (1) hostility toward non-Christian religions, (2) seeing Christianity as the fulfillment of all other religions, and (3) interreligious cooperation.[7] The first attitude is one of antagonism which leads to the denial of validity to the truth claims of other religions, and, in extreme forms, rejects all non-Christian religions as discontinuous with Christianity. The second attitude sees Christianity as the fulfillment of all religions. Other traditions admit of a partial truth as they are illumined by the light of the Christian gospel. The third posture, cooperation, affirms that valid truths are taught in other religions, not simply as they are fulfilled or completed in Christianity. While some examples of this cooperative posture can be found in the church prior to the nineteenth century, Dewick claims that no accredited Christian teacher before that time "openly advocated genuine inter-religious cooperation, based on the readiness to admit that Christianity may have something to receive, as well as to give."[8] Furthermore, in his opinion the first half of the twentieth century has not brought any significant change in attitude: "For the last hundred years the majority of Christian theologians, both in England and on the continent, even when they have shown no active hostility towards non-Christian religions, have tacitly left them out of account, in their anticipations of the future of religion, and have certainly not looked to them for any real contribution towards a wider understanding of truth."[9]

If Dewick's assessment of the attitude of the Christian church toward non-Christian religions by and large is true, then we would have to say that the past twenty-five years represent a departure from precedent. Today, many prominent Christian spokespersons profess an attitude of interreligious cooperation. As F. S. C. Northrop put it, "The unique religious fact of our century is its universal ecumenical mentality."[10] Meetings have been held and publications have appeared from the World Council of Churches Program on Dialogue with People of Living Faiths and Ideologies, and from the Vatican's Secretariat for Non-Christian Religions. Scholarly conferences on truth claims and interreligious dialogue have also been held (e.g., Conference on the Philosophy of Religion, University of Birmingham, 1970). And publications of experts on non-Christian religions, who as committed Christians also write about dialogue with the world's living faiths (e.g., Wilfred Cantwell Smith), all bear witness to a burgeoning interest in this area.


## CONTEMPORARY APPROACHES

Dewick's three categories—discontinuous, fulfillment, and cooperative—adding a fourth, dialogical, which within the past decade has received so much attention, represent the main contemporary approaches of Christians to other faiths. We shall characterize each approach by referring to particular interpreters: Hendrik Kraemer (discontinuous), R. C. Zaehner (fulfillment), cooperative (William E. Hocking), dialogical (Wilfred Cantwell Smith). The last category will receive the greatest elaboration because of its current popularity, and also because our own approach is so indebted to it.[11]

## DISCONTINUITY

The position of discontinuity is well represented by Hendrik Kraemer. Kraemer had been a missionary in the 1920's in Java with the Dutch Bible Society. In reaction to such factors as the increasingly difficult situation of indigenous Christians in an atmosphere of rising Muslim nationalism, and Karl Barth's critique of the 1928 Jerusalem International Missionary Council's position of a common religious front against the evils of secularism, Kraemer became one of the primary spokesmen for a church-centered, evangelistic missiology based on the absolute uniqueness of Christianity. He called for an evangelism based on the "announcement of the Message of God which is not adaptable to any religion or philosophy."[12] Unlike those who would see common features among the experiences and intuitions of religious people, Kraemer insists that the starting point for approaching the non-Christian must be revelation. By this he meant a "given" truth "which is basically different from religious intuition or divination, and which is not a product of human religious consciousness, because according to Biblical religion it enters history in the form of sovereign divine words and acts."[13]

Kraemer's approach argues the absolute uniqueness of Christianity while at the same time not identifying historical Christianity with God's revelation in Christ. All religions express divine-human relationships; however, non-Christian religions are human achievements and must be distinguished from the basic pattern of Christianity which is based on the revelation of Jesus Christ. In *The Christian Message in a Non-Christian World,* Kraemer distinguishes two types of religion: the prophetic religions of revelation and the naturalistic religions of transempirical realization. In the former category he places Christianity, Judaism, and to a certain degree Islam, whereas all other religions fall into the latter category. Even though Judaism and Islam are religions of revelation, historical Christianity is different from them as well as from naturalistic religions. It differs from all other faiths because it "has stood and stands under continuous and direct influence and judgment of the revelation in Christ."[14]

Because the Christian tradition has stood and stands under the continuous and direct influence and judgment of the revelation in Christ, it is essentially different from other religious traditions. Christian history differs qualitatively from secular history and all other religious histories as well. In its most radical form Kraemer's position obviously does not allow for dialogue among Christians and non-Christians, only for witness aimed at conversion. A more moderate stance which Kraemer himself took in his later work, *World Religions and World Cultures*, tends to stress the uniqueness of religious self-understanding in interreligious encounters: "The seriousness of true religion demands that one shall be really one's religious self and avoid the temptation . . . of putting as an indispensable condition of dialogue and relationship the assumption that all religions are essentially one."[15] As we shall see, some representatives of the cooperative approach take the position that Kraemer is attacking.

## FULFILLMENT

Among the best-known representatives of the fulfillment approach to non-Christian religions is R. C. Zaehner, formerly Spalding Professor of Eastern Religion and Ethics at Oxford, whose untimely death cut short a scholarly career of already realized promise. Zaehner is critical of those who enter interreligious dialogue trying to pinpoint the differences between Christianity and non-Christian religions. Such an approach, being essentially negative, is doomed to failure. Consequently, the Christian should approach other religions seeking "to understand them from within and try to grasp how they too seek to penetrate the mystery of our being and our eternal destiny."[16] Exemplifying this sympathetic approach, Zaehner's scholarly studies of non-Christian religions included Hinduism, Buddhism, Islam, Zoroastrianism, and many other traditions.

Zaehner's approach seeks in the first place to find parallels between the Christian tradition and other religious traditions, and consequently see Christianity as the fulfillment or consummation of all other religions. In his analysis of the Indian religious tradition, for example, he notes similarities between the Upanishadic description of the relationship between the soul and God (*Chāndogya*, 3.14) and the thought of the modern Roman Catholic mystic Thomas Merton. More telling, however, is Zaehner's treatment of Indian theism. In the triumph of Krishna devotion in the Bhagavad Gītā and the sequence of Krishna's life in the *Mahābhārata*, he sees a reminder "of the Passion, Resurrection, and Ascension of Our Lord."[17]

Despite Zaehner's efforts to bridge the gap between Christianity and the Indian religious tradition by means of parallels, in the last analysis he is unwilling to treat the two religions as equals. Hence, the message of Krishna in the Bhagavad Gītā "is the message that Christ was later to proclaim *in its fullness.*"[18] In what is perhaps Professor Zaehner's most sweeping statement regarding "the religion of Jesus Christ" as the consummation of other religions he asserts:

> Christ indeed comes to fulfill not only the law and the prophets of Israel, but also the "law and the prophet" of the Āryan race. He fulfills or rounds out the conception of God independently revealed to the Hebrew prophets and to Zoroaster, and by His Crucifixion, Death, Resurrection, and Ascension He points to the type of mystical path the soul must tread if it is to rise beyond the *ātman* or higher self to its predestined reunion with God.[19]

Zaehner's attempt to find a hidden gospel in non-Christian religions or to see the religion of Jesus Christ as the fulfillment of other religions may jeopardize the integrity of interreligious dialogue. What is to keep the devoted Hindu theist from turning the tables and seeing the "religion of Krishna" as the fulfillment of the "religion of Jesus Christ"? Or the Buddhist from seeing the Truth discovered by Siddhartha Gotama as the culmination of the insights taught by Christ? It seems likely that Professor Zaehner's approach, for all of its informed sympathy, leads eventually to the opposition of religious traditions.

## COOPERATION

William E. Hocking, an American philosopher of religion, was a spokesman for an open and cooperative approach to non-Christian religions from the 1930's into the 1950's. His position had been implicitly rejected by Kraemer at the Tambaram conference. In 1940, Hocking tried to meet Kraemer's criticism with the publication of *Living Religions and a World Faith*. Here Hocking argues that religion by its very nature is universal and one, rooted in human nature and belonging to the realm of man's most elemental will.[20] Presuming the universal moral nature of religion leads Hocking to define religion as "a passion for righteousness . . . conceived as a cosmic demand."[21] Religion for Hocking is not mere morality, however. It may underlie morality, but moral codes and customs in and of themselves are culturally relative. Religion, by definition universal in nature, cannot be limited to a particular people or culture. Hence, Hocking's singular proposition is that religion is universal and inherent in all humankind: "There are no natively unreligious peoples or individuals. . . . Religion contains the release from all localisms, and from all historical accidents. It crosses every boundary between man and man, and between the earliest man and the latest in time."[22]

While universal in its essential or *sui generis* nature, religions are also characterized by particularity. The universal must be communicated by means of a particular language, history, and culture. The mystic, who rises above his specific community, finds that he needs his community "with all its particular marks in order to complete his religious self hood."[23] In Hocking's scheme the polarity of the universal and particular is manifested in three types of historic religions: the predominantly local or ethnic; the predominantly universal, arising by an attempt to escape the bonds of the local; the historical-universal, the universal particularized by historic fact.[24]

Within all three of these types of historic religions there is some element of universality. For Hocking, all religions partake of one essence (i.e., the cosmic demand for righteousness): "As any religion grows in its self-understanding through grasping its own essence, it grasps the essence of all religion and gains in power to interpret its various forms."[25] Because all religions can grow toward the religious essence, Hocking speculates that it would be possible for one religion to succeed in incorporating the meaning of all other religions.[26] For Hocking, Christianity in its ideal character anticipates the essence of all religions. It contains potentially all that any one of various historical religions has in actuality.[27] Christianity's universality as a historic religion has not yet reached fulfillment, however. It lacks certain elements contained in other religions, such as the majesty of God in Islam, the reflectiveness of Hinduism, the impersonal element of ultimate truth in Buddhism, and the naturalness of Confucianism. Christianity, nevertheless, is the best qualified to assume leadership in the quest for a world faith. "Its travail through the western phases of modernity has qualified it, and requires it to take a certain leadership in meeting the religious problems of the coming civilization."[28] The problem is not whether Christianity can cast off its Western dress, but whether with its "inescapable biography" it can "present the valid essences of religion [so] as to give them unimpeded force able to meet the issues created everywhere by the abstract universals of the secularized arts and sciences."[29] For Hocking, then, the essence of all religions is a universal righteousness; their plurality is the result of historic accident; Christianity is the supreme religion, not *qualitatively,* but because its history qualifies it to appropriate the fullest meaning of the essence of religion.

## DIALOGUE

Within the past decade one of the most talked about approaches to other religions has been the dialogical, especially in the circles of the World Council of Churches. Dr. Stanley J. Samartha heads a program on Dialogue with People of Living Faiths, and recent World Council publications include *Dialogue Between Men of Living Faiths* and such articles as "Dialogue in Ecumenical History," "Continuing Tasks in Inter-Religious Dialogue," and so on.

What is a dialogical approach to non-Christian religions? First and foremost, dialogue is an encounter of religious persons on the level of their understanding of their deepest commitments and ultimate concerns. I am fully in agreement with Klaus Klostermaier: "By dialogue I do not mean . . . the exchange of views between theologians of different religions. Interesting and necessary as it is, it is not 'dialogue' but 'comparative religion.' The real dialogue is an ultimate personal depth—it need not even be a talking about religious or theological topics. Real dialogues . . . challenge both partners, making them aware of the presence of God, calling both of them to a metanoia from an unknown depth."[30] Or, as he has said in another context, "dialogue is primarily the meeting of human beings. Hindu-Christian dialogue is not so much the meeting between Hinduism and Christianity as between individual Hindus and Christians, each professing his own faith. Dialogue stems, in other words, from a profound recognition of the mutuality of our common life."[31]

On this continent Wilfred Cantwell Smith, now of Dalhousie University, Nova Scotia, and formerly director of the Center for the Study of World Religions at Harvard, has challenged our approach to the study and understanding of religion along dialogical lines as has perhaps no other student of religion. Smith insists that interreligious dialogue and understanding is fundamentally the concern of religious persons. Hence, expressions of personal faith should take priority over analyses of historical traditions. Smith's person-centered approach, like Klaus Klostermaier's, is critical of any approach to religious understanding that transmutes religion into a static system or limits religious life to its historic forms within a particular religious tradition. While Smith is keenly aware of religious traditions qua tradition, his attention is focused on the lives of religious men. Indeed, by his own admission, his approach may be typified as "personalistic."

Smith's focus on religious persons gives his approach an existentialist flavor. He sees the religious person caught fundamentally in the tension of the finite and the infinite, the mundane and the transmundane. In his own words, the life of the religious man is suspended between the tension of "the mundane realm of limiting and observable and changing actuality and a realm transcending this."[32] This unresolved polarity lies at the heart of religious metaphysical and theological systems.

In Professor Smith's view the study of man's religions in the past has been inadequate because it has not properly understood the polar nature of religion. It has focused on either the mundane or the transmundane pole or "has been confused in so far as its concept has attempted to embrace both."[33] Neither side can be omitted, yet they cannot be combined, because they are different realities. Smith suggests that for purposes of analysis they be separated. To make the separation necessitates the elimination of the single concept, "religion," and the substitution of two concepts, "faith" and "tradition" (or "cumulative tradition"). By faith he means "an inner religious experience or involvement of a particular person; the impingement on him of the transcendent putative or real."[34] Thus faith, for Smith, is that dimension of human experience in touch with the nonobservable real beyond changing actuality. By tradition he means the cumulative "mass of overt objective data that constitute the historical deposit . . . of the past religious life of the community in question."[35] With this distinction Professor Smith hopes, on the one hand, to avoid the pitfall of making religion merely a system of doctrines and practices and, on the other hand, to ensure that the student of religion will do justice to religions as historical phenomena (both collective and personal) while at the same time recognizing that they are not entirely limited by history.

On one level, Smith's use of the two categories, faith and tradition, is simply a criticism of traditional ways of understanding religion. More profoundly, however, this criticism is rooted in a particular understanding of the pattern of man's religiousness.[36] Religion, fundamentally, is a way of life. The religious life is basic to the kind of relationship an individual has to himself, his fellowmen, and the ground of his existence. In Smith's view, at its most basic level the religious life introduces the individual to that which is without limits.[37] In applying this proposition to Christianity one might characterize the Christian life as a new life on a supernatural level.[38] Because the religious life is oriented to ultimate reality or, in other words, is lived on a supernatural level, religion is not to be taken simply as *one* aspect of a person's life. It is, rather, a total, comprehensive way of participating in or looking at all of life. From this perspective Smith describes a religious reformer as one who seeks not to reform a religion but to reform men's awareness of their total environment.[39]

Professor Smith's description of religion as a way of life in relationship to that which is without limits has similarities to Joachim Wach's characterization of religious experience as a total response to one's whole being to the unlimited ultimate reality.[40] For both scholars, various observable expressions of religion—e.g., doctrinal and moral systems, religious communities—are rooted in religious experience. As we have seen, for Smith personal faith is inner religious experience, and its expressions include art, community, "character," ritual and morality, ideas and words.[41] It is important to keep in mind that in Smith's approach, as in the approach of Joachim Wach, all aspects of the overt historical tradition are properly understood only in relationship to religious experience or, for Smith, faith. Thus, regarding religious statements Smith says, "The proper way to understand a religious statement is to endeavour . . . to see what [its words and clauses] meant to the man who first uttered them, and what they have meant to those since for whom they have served as *expressions of their faith.*"[42]

The essence of religion, for Smith, is the life of personal faith. A religious tradition functions as the context in which faith may arise. At its best, tradition is a channel of the religious life. At its worst, it obstructs religious vitality or serves as a pseudo faith.[43] Correspondingly, when one studies religion, the religious tradition at its best may reveal the true significance of the life of faith. At its worst, however, it may serve to obstruct "what the universe means to the religious man."[44]

Given the nature of religion, it becomes impossible to define either religion in general or a particular religion. A particular religion is not simply a historical tradition or the way in which the historical tradition has understood itself but a way of looking at the entire universe. For this reason a religion is difficult to conceptualize. On the one hand, it is a rich variety of factors comprehending all of life; on the other, every facet can be properly understood only in relationship to faith, that inner experience which links man to the ultimately real beyond any limitation, even the qualification of concept.

Professor Smith's approach to interreligious dialogue has a great appeal in its emphasis on religion as a way of life rather than as a static system. This stance makes interreligious dialogue a dynamic experience, an experience of becoming as a religious person and not merely of knowing or learning about. Thus, Smith states:

> I believe that there is a relation between a man's own personal faith and his understanding of the religious life of other men. I think that each is relevant to the other, and that it ought to be relevant. . . . Interreligious understanding is not merely an intellectual or academic or "objective" question. To ask about other men's faith is in itself to raise important issues about one's own.[45]

Smith's position, while appealing, is not without its problems. Whereas we can appreciate the thrust of his concern over the barrenness of the "ism" approach to the study of religion, the nature of the distinction between the categories of faith and tradition is not entirely clear. On the one hand, they appear to be irreconcilable poles. Yet, if personal faith —i.e., religious experience—expresses itself through varying aspects of the cumulative tradition, then how can the two be separated? As Ninian Smart cogently remarks, even mystics whose experience of ultimate reality is inexpressible "go on to speak about religion in terms of the formulations of their own faith!"[46] How does one go about separating the language of faith from the inner experience of the religious person?

The ambiguity of the relationship between personal faith and the cumulative tradition in Smith's approach creates some difficult problems. In his Taylor lectures delivered at Yale Divinity School in 1963, Professor Smith makes the claim that the Christianity of one man may be "more true" than that of another. He also says, "I also have two Muslim friends, of whom the religion of one is more true than the religion of the other."[47] But on what grounds can Smith make such a judgment? He has claimed that religious truth

lies only in persons ("The only question that concerns either
God or me, or my neighbor is whether *my* Christianity is
true, and whether *yours* is").[48] Given such an understanding
of religious truth, by what criterion can he judge the religiousness of one man over another other than by his own
private experience or by the testimony of the parties involved? John Hick sees a similar problem in Smith's personalistic theory of truth. While acknowledging the truth and
importance of Smith's position, Hick argues that it still leaves
us with the "problem of the relation between the truth-
claims of the different religions that become true in the lives
of their sincere adherents. For surely 'Christianity' or 'Islam'
or 'Hinduism' can only *become* true in the personalistic sense
because they are already true in another, more universal and
objective though less existential sense."[49]

A similar problem emerges when Professor Smith states
that the terms "true" and "false" do not refer to some
sort of prototype of a particular religious tradition but "to
the prototype of what religion ought to be."[50] From
Smith's personalistic stance, does the prototype of what
religion ought to be not run the danger of being what *I*
think religion ought to be? If so, then Smith's approach to
interreligious dialogue might tend to pit one person's religious experience against another's just as R. C. Zaehner's
approach would seem to juxtapose religious traditions.

## CONDITIONS FOR DIALOGUE

Having examined three approaches to non-Christian religions selectively rather than exhaustively, and studied more
thoroughly the dialogical stance of Wilfred Cantwell Smith,
I shall now outline my own stance around five topics. Collec-
tively they do not set forth a complete theory of the relationships between religious traditions; rather, they characterize
what I like to think of as necessary conditions for interreligious dialogue.

## BEING ENGAGED BY THE FAITH OF THE OTHER

Those who approach non-Christian religions as sensitively and sympathetically as Klaus Klostermaier or the late Trappist monk, Thomas Merton, illustrate one of the first requisites for a dialogue. It is the necessity of *being engaged by the faith of the other*. Nothing significant emerges out of dialogue unless we have been seriously tested, challenged, and enticed by the faith stance of our partners in dialogue. If we approach people of other religious persuasions purely from the standpoint of advocacy, if we believe that our particular perception of religious truth is the *only* correct one, then genuine dialogue does not take place. What occurs is merely a series of monologues. Then we are unable to participate in the meaning that religious truth claims have for others, nor are we open enough to allow those claims to affect us. Such a situation is like a number of seminar discussions I have heard. Student A proposes a thesis, student B makes a response. However, often student B's response is only tangentially related to the proposed thesis. Rather than try to encounter the thesis or further elucidate the meaning intended by student A who proposed it, student B is much more interested in getting his own ideas in front of his fellow students. No genuine dialogue takes place in such discussions, and there is no real mutual sharing of ideas. Consequently, intellectual growth is truncated. In a similar manner, when interreligious "dialogue" in fact becomes a series of monologues, religious insight is stunted. The mutual sharing of religious convictions ought to be a major arena for spiritual growth whether the context is inter-Christian or interreligious. To be so defensive about the advocacy of our own convictions that we fail to appreciate the convictions of another produces a staleness in our own religiousness.

## ADEQUATE RELIGIOUS SELF-UNDERSTANDING

A second requisite for a theology of dialogue relates closely to the first. A willingness to be engaged by the truth claims of the other person demands openness, to be sure, but it also calls for an *awareness of the uniqueness of one's own faith.* Just as a wedding engagement by necessity involves two parties, a theology of dialogue develops from the engagement or encounter of two or more distinctive religious positions. Openness without the fulcrum of prior religious self-awareness or faith commitments can weigh nothing in the balance. It is like sewing a piece of cloth with no knot in the thread. One sews and sews, but no seam results. In the end, one is left with the separate pieces of cloth, thread and needle. Without a point of view or faith perspective, a theology of dialogue is formless, an unrelated collection of disparate parts. Syncretism at its worst scissors-and-pastes together a theology. Such a theological composite takes a bit from this tradition and a bit from that with nothing to tie them together but the good intentions of being open-minded.

A dialogical approach to religious understanding does not produce such a syncretistic composite. The religious person is open to the truth claims of the other because he himself has made ultimate commitments and has experienced the significance and meaning of such commitments in his own life. How does one convey color to one who is blind or sound to one who is deaf unless one has reflected on the experience of color or sound? Or, how does one denote the meaning of love to one who has not loved or been loved? I am reminded of a college friend who, one evening, was ecstatically describing his feeling for his girl friend. I was aware of two reactions to his outpouring of emotion. On the one hand, I could sense the deep meaning behind his words because I had experienced similar feelings; on the other hand, because of the deeply personal and private nature of this experience neither he nor I could capture this meaning adequately in words. I was open to the experience of my friend and could, to a limited degree, understand his feelings because I had known them myself. In a similar manner the religious man is able to find meaning in the faith of a friend because of his own faith commitments.

I once overheard a heated discussion between two Protestant missionaries in the Near East. One argued that modern Israel promised to be a fruitful missionary field because such a large percentage of Jews migrating to Israel were basically secular. The other argued that the secular Jew would have less understanding of the nature of religious commitment and would be a poorer prospect for conversion. From the perspective of dialogue the debate misplaces the issue. The point is not whether a person of secular or religious background responds more favorably to evangelistic appeals, but whether an individual's witness of faith through his tradition creates an environment where religious self-understanding deepens and matures.

The same point can be applied to the interest among many Buddhists in establishing missions in the West. I have heard several comment that because of the secularism and materialism in the West, Buddhism has a promising future in such countries as the United States. Without our disputing the claim about the current spiritual state of Western society, a dialogical perspective would suggest that Buddhist missions to the West should be less concerned about the *number* of conversions to Buddhism and more interested in affecting the quality of religious life regardless of the particular religious label one wears. In a similar vein, one of my Sinhalese Christian friends who teaches Christian education at the Roman Catholic seminary in Kandy has said that part of the mission of the Christian church in Sri Lanka should be to make Buddhists better Buddhists. Such a suggestion may sound like nonsense or even heresy. Yet, in terms of a dialogical approach where religious men with deep conviction encounter one another with the openness to be moved to new dimensions of faith, such a proposal makes perfectly good sense.

Both religious self-understanding and openness are requisites for genuine and meaningful interreligious dialogue. Others are a thoughtful reconsideration of what we mean by the terms "religion" and "truth."

### RETHINKING DEFINITIONS

We have seen how Wilfred Cantwell Smith calls for a reconsideration of the term "religion" and suggests that a more phenomenologically accurate set of terms would be "cumulative tradition" and "personal faith." Smith's strong personalistic faith emphasis has been criticized on the grounds that the faith/tradition or faith/doctrine distinction creates more problems than it solves. Still his general concern for breaking out of definitional stereotypes and his emphasis on the priority of an individual's faith stance are useful for honest and open dialogue. An individual Christian has a faith stance peculiarly his own precisely because he is a unique person with a distinctive set of experiences. His experience is not isolated, however. His faith has been formed within the context of a historical tradition broadly defined as Christian and more narrowly labeled as Italian Catholic, American Presbyterian, Swedish Lutheran, and so on. Correspondingly, we can say that an individual Buddhist has an inner religious experience or faith uniquely formed through the prism of his own experience but within the context of a historical religious community such as Thai Theravāda Buddhism.

Understanding our religious identification in terms of faith and tradition rather than simply as Buddhist or Christian greatly clarifies the religious situation and facilitates dialogue. My own inner personal religious experience is not precisely identical with any of my Christian brethren past or present. My relationship with my family, denominational background, teen-age crises, education, study of Buddhism, etc., have all conditioned my own religious self-awareness. At the deepest level of my being, Christian symbols have a meaning peculiar to this inner experience. On the cognitive level, furthermore, I will express my faith in an idiom or vocabulary which best expresses that inner experience. For example, the Buddhist concept of *anattā*, or not-self, elucidates for me the Christian concept of the New Creation in Christ. In terms of my faith these concepts are internally consistent. I am aware, moreover, that my faith is externally more consistent with some strands of the historic tradition of Christianity than others. In other words, I feel more at home with some parts of the Christian tradition than with others. For example, I am more comfortable with Augustine than Aquinas, and with Paul Tillich than Karl Barth. What I have here observed of myself applies to every other religious person whatever his or her religious persuasion.

From the perspective of faith and tradition, religious dialogue can be more honestly carried out. When my Buddhist friend discusses Buddhism he will, on the one hand, be representing his own faith and, on the other, certain aspects of the historic deposit of the Buddhist tradition. His personal faith in the Buddha, for example, may be more consistent with the historical Buddhist concept of the great man *(mahāpurisa)* but less consistent with the concept of *sattha*, or teacher. Correspondingly, my own view of Jesus Christ may be more consistent with the suffering servant motif of Second Isaiah rather than the cosmological savior of Philippians. Both of us are acknowledging in this kind of approach the richness and variety which our religious traditions represent. They are unique but are part of ongoing, common traditions. Also our faiths as well as our traditions are rooted in truth claims whose ultimacy engenders them with value and power.

It is precisely the ultimacy or absoluteness of religious truth claims whether as an expression of faith or of tradition which leads to the fourth requisite for a theology of dialogue

*—a reconsideration of the meaning of absolute or ultimate truth.* Such a reconsideration is necessary since, as Dewick argues, the missionary enterprise has until quite recently based its exclusive approach to non-Christian religions on the grounds that the Christian revelation in Jesus Christ is the Absolute Truth and that all other religious truth claims are only varying degrees of relative truth. We have seen such an approach suggested by Hendrik Kraemer in *A Christian Message in a Non-Christian World.* While the Christian holds the Christ event to be normative for his faith, does its absoluteness negate the validity of the truth claims of other religions? Such an understanding may be based more on the logic of metaphysics then on the logic of faith. It may be indebted more to a Greek understanding of God as Absolute Truth than to the Biblical view of God whose truth is never a matter of definition but of encounter or relationship within the context of the human situation.

## TRUTH AS RELATIONSHIP

Too often throughout the history of the Christian church the Bible's understanding of truth as God's involvement in human history has become reduced to a set of unchanging propositions. In other words, the truth which cannot be named becomes circumscribed by the creeds and confessions of the church or by our own limited understanding. Such a limitation of God's truth is contrary to the Biblical tradition.

The Genesis story of Adam and Eve's desire to know God may be interpreted as an illustration of man's quest to be like God, but also of man's inveterate tendency to pull God down to his own level; to limit God by knowing him on human terms alone. Yahweh's appearance to Moses on Sinai emphasizes the truth that God cannot be circumscribed by an image. In the Gospel of John, the identification of Jesus the Christ with the universal Logos or Word is one way the New Testament underscores the fact that God is not limited to legal or linguistic norms. Though the Genesis story of the Garden of Eden, the Exodus account of Moses' receipt of God's law, and the Johannine identification of the Greek Logos with Jesus are very different in form, their contexts point to common meaning. The Eden event distinguishes man's limited knowledge from God's omniscience; the Moses event lifts the Israelites beyond the limitations of idols; and the Christ event elevates the Christian community beyond the bounds of Jewish law. On the levels of myth, legend, and history these Biblical perspectives point to a liberating and, hence, universalizing truth. They establish man's highest end and his most complete fulfillment not in relationship to any particular object (e.g., an idol) or to any particular definition of behavior (e.g., the Mosaic law) but in relationship to that which is beyond particularization and beyond definition, i.e., God. God's truth as absolute and universal means that God is the "I Am Who I Am," the name beyond every name, the ground of existence whose very nature is its *unqualifiedness*.

In the Biblical tradition, truth emerges from man's relationship with this unqualified and unlimited ground of existence. It is concrete and particular in that each person must confront the truth in his actual, living situation; yet it is absolute and universal in that the truth is, within itself, not subject to any limitation or circumscription. For the Christian the incarnation embodies the fact that truth is relationship and here in the depths of humanity is the perfect expression of divinity.

To borrow a phrase from Martin Buber, the Jewish theologian of dialogue, Jesus is within himself the perfected "I-Thou" relationship. He is what every man can become—a son of God (Gospel of John) or a New Adam (I Corinthians) —who has realized the truth in his own being. The Christian's claim that Jesus is the truth is a way of saying that the truth is non-propositional and that Jesus made that truth manifest.

To understand the truth as the perfected relationship between man and God brings a judgment to bear on my own perception of truth. For the Christian, Jesus Christ is this perfected relationship. He is the truth. To the degree that I embody the same relationship—to the degree I am a Christ person—to that degree I am also the truth; however, the opposite also holds. To the degree that my relationship to God is obstructed by my own blindness and shortcoming, to that degree I fail to perceive the truth. Consequently, my perception of truth is enhanced whenever my own untruth is diminished. Such spiritual or religious growth often occurs when I encounter religious men whose ultimate concern is deeper than my own. Thus it happens that my own faith may be more enhanced or my perception of the truth more perfected through dialogue with religious traditions or adherents of those traditions other than my own. Or, to use the symbols of the Christian tradition, Christlikeness (i.e., the perfected relationship between man and God) is not confined within the walls of the institutional Christian church, nor within its confessional statements.

Precisely because the truth knows no institutional or confessional boundaries, interreligious dialogue is an imperative. The truth in a religious sense is not confined to the syllogisms of logic, the propositions of metaphysics, or the calculus of mathematics. Rather, it emerges from the dialogue between man and that which claims his ultimate loyalty or concern. From the perspective of dialogue the Christian can share his own faith or her ultimate concern without having to see the faith of a Buddhist colleague as being inferior or less true. Quite the contrary, it now becomes possible for the Christian to find in the perfection of the faith of the other a challenge to his or her own self-awareness as a religious person. From this perspective, dialogue must now be seen as imperative, a fifth requisite of a theology of dialogue.

## THE IMPERATIVE OF DIALOGUE

For the Christian the incarnation makes dialogue imperative. In the incarnation the divine identifies with all aspects of human life. Ultimate truth particularizes itself in concrete form not to become limited but to confront man face-to-face. Similarly, those who would share the Christian gospel must enter into the idiom of particular situations, as did the apostle Paul, who confessed to the Corinthians, "I have become all things to all men" (I Cor. 9:22). Becoming all things to all men means substantiating one's faith by seeking the truth in concrete situations. The Christian does not possess the truth; rather, he possesses faith—that posture of absolute commitment or ultimate concern which makes him open to the ultimate truth as it reveals itself in particular encounters. The Christian does not possess Christ; he seeks Christ in actual, living situations. God in dialogue with the world makes his word (Logos) into a concrete reality; the Christian continually actualizes his faith through genuine dialogue with his neighbor. Perhaps a modern parable will best illustrate this point:

Two men were seated together in a train compartment riding from Oxford to London. One was middle-aged and slightly heavyset, with a certain bearing of wise experience. The other was younger, with a tense, rather aggressive air. The older man tried several times to engage the younger man in conversation but with no results. The latter either sat immobile in deep concentration or jotted notes on a pad of paper held in his hand. As the train reached its destination the younger man finally broke out of his silence and introduced himself as an Oxford student headed for a debate in London on Britain's entry into the common market. The older man smiled, wished him well in the debate, and said he was sorry he would not have a chance to hear it but that he was going to a meeting at the Prime Minister's on the same subject. "You see," he said, "I have been responsible for drafting our common market negotiations." Too often like the young debater we close ourselves off to unprecedented opportunity in the realm of the spirit as well as the world. In the posture of dialogue, faith discovers truth. From this discovery we grow as religious persons.

*Chapter 2*

# In the World
# But Not of It

"Humanity, I love you. You're always putting the secret of life in your hip pocket, forgetting it's there, and sitting down on it!" With words like these, the American poet e. e. cummings has paraphrased the modern human condition. We have sat down so often on the secret of life that we seem nearly unable to recover it. Bloodshed and armed conflict abound in many parts of the world. Pollution of air and water endangers not only health but life itself. The world's energy resources are being consumed beyond our capacity to rebuild. Respect and consideration, love and mercy seem to be overcome by the drive of acquisitive self-interest. Mores and morals are displaced and disrupted by rapid social change. In the well-phrased words of William Wordsworth, "The world is too much with us; late and soon, Getting and spending, we lay waste our powers."

Neither poet has, perhaps, done quite as good a job of capturing the predicament of the world as the writer of the Gospel of Matthew: "Do not lay up for yourselves treasures on earth, where moth and rust consume and where thieves break in and steal" (Matt. 6:19). The writers of both the Old and New Testaments treated the world with varying degrees of suspicion. While the world of affairs was created by God, it was still a battleground of loyalties. The Genesis story of the Fall symbolized in the person of the serpent the power in the world opposing God's will; and the Old Testament historical and prophetic writings provide a classic record of conflicting commitments. Indeed, the Old Testament is as much a story of the Israelites' disobedience to God as of their obedience!

The Synoptic Gospels gave a particular thrust or interpretation to the Old Testament theme of conflict. From the exilic and post-exilic writings like The Book of Daniel the Synoptic writers saw the world as a conflict of two times, ages, or aeons. Jesus Christ arrives as the originator of the new age.

The present time is a between-time, the time begun by the advent of Jesus and to be concluded by his second coming. The person of the between-time lives in the present in the expectation of a future promise. In brief, the Synoptic writers were oriented toward a yet to be fulfilled hope. This orientation gives the Old Testament theme of conflict an even greater urgency: the time of fulfillment is at hand; concerns of the world must be dismissed or relegated to a subsidiary place. Both the Synoptic writers and Paul live under this end-time perspective. It affects their attitudes toward many aspects of worldly activity including ethical behavior, the relationship between the Christian and government, and the nature of the church in the world. We shall briefly examine the New Testament eschatological (end-time) perspective in terms of these topics, and then make some general comparisons with the perspective of the institutional church in the modern period. Then we shall examine a classical Theravāda Buddhist attitude toward the world to see how contemporary Christian reflection on the nature of the world might recapture the essential meaning of the New Testament's end-time perspective on the world.

## ESCHATOLOGY AND ETHICS

A person who looks to the New Testament to provide a systematic guide for practical behavior in the world will be disappointed. No such ethical handbook is found between its covers. Instead, in the Synoptics one finds an ethic of right moral discrimination rather than prescription, and in Paul's letters situational advice appropriate to particular problems of the young churches. In the Synoptics the Sermon on the Mount (Matt. 5:1–12) stands out as the most widely known section of ethical materials. These chapters in Matthew have inspired both Christians and non-Christians alike. Mahatma Gandhi is reputed to have embraced the Sermon on the Mount as containing some of the most noble ethical sentiments in the world's religious literature. But what kind of ethical program does the Sermon on the Mount give us?

Unlike the specific commandments in the Mosaic Law code of Exodus, the Sermon on the Mount blesses people who are "poor in spirit," "meek," and "peacemakers." Although such terms do indeed denote an ethical posture or an attitude informing behavior, they do not provide a program of ethics. This ethical posture or attitude is one that emphasizes right moral perception, attitude, and understanding. As Amos Wilder observes, Jesus appeals to moral discernment rather than the law.[1] Remember for a moment Jesus' admonition against the Pharisees for their hypocritical pride in the performance of pious acts (Matt. 23:13–15), or his praise of the poor widow even though the amount she donated to the temple was quite small (Luke 21:2), or his challenge that adulterous thoughts are as condemnable as the adulterous act itself (Matt. 5:27–28). All three cases celebrate righteousness or ethical goodness in terms of right moral discernment rather than obedience to an external norm. It is, of course, expected that good deeds will result—"A good tree bears good fruit"—but true ethical goodness is a quality of one's very being rather than an enumeration of good deeds. Goodness cannot be measured by outer acts but is a matter of inner character.

The Synoptic Gospels do provide us with a few specific ethical situations. There is the story of the good Samaritan (Luke 10:29–37) which not only praises people who go out of their way to help those in need but is also a lesson in race relations. The Samaritan who stopped to help the man by the side of the road was a member of a race looked down upon by the Jews. This story contains some specific ethical advice, to be sure. It also exemplifies the general rule that neighborliness or humaneness demands that we offer a helping hand to those in need. Yet the striking fact about this story is not the general maxim that the Christian *should* help those in need but rather that the Christian helps those in need without reservation, hesitation, or calculation as a matter of his very being. At no point does the Samaritan pause to consider whether his status as a Samaritan should qualify his action, nor does he debate whether he should be out of pocket for the man's room and board at the inn. How does one develop this reflex action of self-giving love and concern? The story is silent at this point.

The ethics or the ethical posture of Jesus might be characterized as an eschatological ethic, an ethic of the present kingdom of God, or a new covenant ethics. They are eschatological in the sense of their urgency, that Jesus signals a new religious situation which offers a new order of relationships and responsibilities. The conditions of the ethical life are now changed. No longer is the model one of servants to the law but of sons of God: "The new situation is . . . the anticipated time of salvation in which men are no longer hard-hearted, in which they become God's sons in a full sense."[2] The tension in the ethical attitude of Jesus stems from his sense of the uniqueness and significance of his task and the corresponding resistance from the old order governing the world. The radical nature of the eschatological ethic in the Synoptics does not depend so much on the fact of the "imminence of the final revelation and on the fortuitous shortness of the term, but on the essential factor that the conjuncture for which men must prepare is the Kingdom of God."[3] The ethics of Jesus, then, are a sign of a new age or a new order just as surely as is the person of the Christ himself. A new religious situation, a time of salvation, signaled by the person of Jesus, has emerged. It calls for a new righteousness, not one under burden of the law, but the yoke of lowliness and gentleness (Matt. 11:28–30).

Paul's letters, like the Gospels, are not of much greater help in providing a systematic ethical program. Paul's ethical posture has been characterized by George F. Thomas as an "ethic of redemption." Victor P. Furnish notes that Paul's eschatological perspective provides the key to understanding Paul's theology and his ethics. "While Paul does exhort, instruct, admonish, and advise his readers, this is almost always done in an *ad hoc* fashion in relation to specific situations and cases. No single practical ethical pattern of 'Christian code of conduct' is ever promulgated. He sponsors no particular ethical program, and his various specific ethical injunctions taken together are not intended to provide a comprehensive portrait of 'the Christian man.' "[4] Furnish argues that the peculiar character of the Pauline ethic is dominated by three motifs: theological, eschatological, and Christological. If we take them together, we can see how his ethical posture might be characterized fundamentally as redemptive. The Pauline ethic is radically *theo*logical because it "presupposed that man's whole life and being is dependent upon the sovereign, creative, and redemptive power of God." It is eschatological because the sovereignty of God's power is expressed in the temporal terms of God's future triumph over all hostile powers. It is Christological because Christ's humility and selfless love affirmed in his death and resurrection make available the grace through which God's power is activated in the world.[5] Thus, Paul exhorts the Christian to be sanctified in the sense of being holy: "I appeal to you therefore, brethren, by the mercies of God, to present your bodies as a living sacrifice, holy and acceptable to God, which is your spiritual worship. Do not be conformed to this world but be transformed by the renewal of your mind, that you may prove what is the will of God, what is good and acceptable and perfect" (Rom. 12:1–2).

Paul's eschatological ethical posture when applied to specific cases evidences how radically one is to be transformed. For example, in his letter to the Corinthians he advises against marriage because a married person has more worldly concerns than an unmarried person: "I mean, brethren, the appointed time has grown very short; from now on, let those who have wives live as though they had none, and those who mourn as though they were not mourning, and those who rejoice as though they were not rejoicing, and those who buy as though they had no goods, and those who deal with the world as though they had no dealings with it. For the form of this world is passing away" (I Cor. 7:29–31). The new age dictates that Christians are to act in a way that seems almost otherworldly. Married life, mourning, rejoicing, buying and selling—indeed all relations with the world—are transformed. The world as we know it is passing away; consequently, one acts in the world without any attachment to the action itself, but with single-minded attention to a higher goal. Much like the Chinese sage, Lao-tzu, who advocated acting non-actively *(wu wei)*, or the Bhagavad Gītā of Hinduism which proposed an ethic transcending consequences *(karma yoga)*, the apostle Paul argues for action not calculated according to worldly norms—deal with the world as though you had no dealings with it! The Christian is hard pressed to find a program of general social ethics here!

## THE CHURCH AND THE WORLD

The New Testament also offers only sporadic direction regarding the Christian's role in the political structure. Matthew's perspective is one of divided loyalties—"Render . . . to Caesar the things that are Caesar's, and to God the things that are God's" (Matt. 22:21). Paul advocates submission to political power on the grounds that all authority rests ultimately with God (Rom. 13:1) but also because of the nearness of the end-time: "Salvation is nearer to us now than when we first believed; the night is far gone, the day is at hand" (Rom. 13:11b–12a). For Paul the Christian must live *in* the world but not be *of* the world. As we have seen, he is not to be conformed to the world but to be transformed by the renewal of his mind. A stance of distance from the state also characterized the early church until its adoption as the official religion of the Holy Roman Empire by the emperor Constantine, in the fourth century A.D. For this reason religious martyrdom for failure to submit to the state was a very real experience to the early church and coincided with Christ's own sacrificial death at the hands of political authorities. Ignatius, bishop of Antioch, suffered martyrdom during the reign of the emperor Trajan in the second century A.D. Writing to the Christians in Rome, Ignatius says: "Come fire and cross and grappling with wild beasts, wrenching of bones, hacking of limbs, crushing of my whole body. . . . Only be it mine to attain unto Jesus Christ. . . . Bestow not upon the world one who desireth to be God's, neither allure him with material things. Suffer me to receive the pure light. . . . Permit me to be an imitator of the passion of my God."[6] Divided loyalties, submission to the state for reasons of the approaching eschaton, martyrdom—these were some of the themes characterizing the early church's relationship to the state.

The New Testament depicts Christ's followers as people who have severed ordinary and expected relationships with the world. There is no time to plow another furrow or even to bury one's father (Matt. 8:22). Now is the time to deny oneself, take up the cross of abnegation, and follow Jesus (Mark 8:34). The church is a body of people waiting in anticipation of an imminent fulfillment to the signs evidenced in the living and dying of Jesus. Thus, in writing to the Corinthians, Paul admonishes the people to cast the morally impure man from their midst rather than be contaminated by him. Harsh words, to be sure, but consistent with Paul's expectation of the imminent fulfillment of time and the need to prepare for this end.

The consequence of the New Testament expectation of the fullness of time is a life not bound up with worldly preoccupations: "Do not be anxious about your life, what you shall eat, nor about your body, what you shall put on. For life is more than food, and the body more than clothing. . . . Do not seek what you are to eat and what you are to drink, nor be of anxious mind. For all the nations of the world seek these things; and your Father knows that you need them. Instead, seek his kingdom, and these things shall be yours as well" (Luke 12:22–23, 29–31). It is difficult to live in the world and not be anxious about the necessities of life; yet the elimination of such worldly concerns is one of the consequences of the New Testament attitude toward the world. Such a viewpoint has been difficult for the institutional church to maintain. On the other hand, such a critical attitude toward the world is necessary if the church is to avoid becoming simply one social organization among many.

I have briefly outlined several aspects of the eschatological underpinning of the Synoptic Gospels and Paul's letters. Do they characterize the contemporary church around the world today? Is the Christian church continually being revitalized by the early church's critical perspective on the world or is it too closely identified with the goals of its cultural societies? In the nineteenth century Søren Kierkegaard, a famous Danish theologian, made a distinction between "Christianity" and "Christendom." Christianity was the ideal teaching and practice of the tradition. Christendom was this ideal institutionalized and acculturated. Of the latter, Kierkegaard wrote, "Christendom in Denmark dances to the tune, 'Merrily We Roll Along.' " Again, in a master stroke of double irony, Kierkegaard describes a high official in the Danish church who ascends the pulpit in a magnificent cathedral to preach with emotion on the text "God hath elected the base things of the world and the things that are despised." And, says Kierkegaard, "nobody laughs."[7] The juxtaposition of the splendor of the cathedral and the sermon text is biting irony, but to add the note that the congregation did not even perceive the irony jabs the point home even farther. The church in Denmark had become so closely identified with the world that Kierkegaard thought it no longer embodied Christ's teachings.

William James, the famous American philosopher and psychologist of the early part of this century, was another person suspicious of institutionalized religion. He looked upon Sunday Christians as those for whom religion was a "dull habit" rather than an "acute fever." For James, real religion was lived at the level of individual religious experience. Religion as a matter largely of cultural or group identification does not, said James, provide the focal point for ultimate commitment that transforms one's life. Do religious institutions succeed in embodying the ideal teachings of their founders? Too often they tend to entropy, to become encrusted with tradition, to become too closely identified with a particular culture or too closely identified with secular goals and aspirations. In the first quarter of this century, for example, the central Protestant traditions in America embraced a viewpoint that identified the kingdom of God with a kingdom in the process of being built on earth. A far cry from the New Testament's suspicion of the present age.

There is, of course, a different perspective on institutional religion which would challenge both James's tendency to extrapolate religion into religious experience as well as the interpretation in this chapter of the eschatological thrust of early Christianity. From a Durkheimian or sociology of religion point of view religion is a human creation for the maintenance of an objective social reality: "the establishment, through human activity, of an all-embracing sacred order, that is, of a sacred cosmos that will be capable of maintaining itself in the ever-present face of chaos."[8] The perspective taken here is somewhat different. Of course, religions such as

early Christianity and early Indian Buddhism developed
within the cultures of Europe and India and bear the marks
of those cultural societies; however, I would agree with H.
Richard Niebuhr *(Christ and Culture)* and Robert Bellah
("Religion and Progress in Modern Asia") that they are not
bound by their cultural and historical heritages. Both appeal
to the universal nature of their founders' teaching, and both
traditions have a critical understanding of the secular or
mundane world. Yet, because religions become institutionalized within a particular culture, they tend to adopt not only
the form but the goals of that culture. Paradoxical as it may
seem, when a religious tradition "succeeds," measured in
terms of secular institutions, at that point its appeal to a
higher or transcendent goal is endangered. Furthermore, its
critical posture toward the expectations and goals of its cultural society is jeopardized. How does a religious tradition
avoid becoming overly acculturated, particularized, parochi-
alized, and secularized? In the case of Christianity how does
the New Testament's suspicion of the worldly customs and
behavior embodied in its end-time (eschatological) hope
avoid becoming so diluted and compromised that an essential Biblical insight is destroyed? Or, in the terms of Bishop
Gustavo Gutiérrez, how does theology retain its role as critical reflection on *praxis?*[9]

A theology of dialogue provides one kind of answer. The
Christian can engage a religious tradition like Buddhism in
such a manner that particular perspectives within it provide
new insight into the New Testament attitude toward the
world. In my opinion, one finds just such an opportunity in
the Buddhist teaching of *anicca,* or impermanence. Keep in
mind that I am not arguing for a syncretism of Christian and
Buddhist views. Rather, I am encouraging the Christian to
appreciate anew the importance of one theme in his own
tradition's understanding of the world through openness
to another religious tradition. We shall briefly examine the
Theravāda view of the world, and then use the insight gained

to reexamine the New Testament's eschatological perspective on the world.

## BUDDHISM—
## IMPERMANENCE AND CONDITIONED GENESIS

One of the fundamental teachings of Buddhism is that the sensate world is not as it appears to be to most men. We attribute to both persons and objects a permanent and unchanging character they really do not have. Thus, we perceive tables and chairs to have an enduring quality of stability and hardness, people to be possessed of a personality or selfhood underlying their changing attributes, and social and political institutions to embody a character that prevails in the face of the winds of time. On the basis of such perceptions we attempt to structure our own secure world. We build a family, a vocation, a nation-state on the assumption that they will last—at least for the duration of our own lifetime. In short we root our lives in attachment to the things of this world. Buddhism sees such attachment as a condition of ignorance leading to suffering and unhappiness because attachment is based on the error that things exist independently and enduringly rather than interdependently and fleetingly. In fact, the mundane world exists only in the dynamic process of coming into existence and going out of existence. Consequently, he who sees things as they really are in the process of continually becoming and fading away grasps at nothing (*Samyutta-Nikāya*, II. 47). He becomes free, unattached.

A thirsty, weary traveler looks down the hot, dusty road and sees the dancing rivulets of a crystal stream. It is a mirage, of course, but to his parched lips and eyes it appears to be real. He runs to plunge his body into the water but upon reaching the spot he discovers that the stream has disappeared. Buddhism sees the world as a mirage, not that it does not exist or is unreal, but that we misperceive it through our various wrong attachments:

> All things, O priests, are on fire. . . .
> The eye, O priests, is on fire; forms are on fire; eye-consciousness is on fire; impressions received by the eye are on fire; and whatever sensation, pleasant, unpleasant, or indifferent, originates in dependence on impressions received by the eye, that also is on fire.
> And with what are these on fire?
> With the fire of passion, say I, with the fire of hatred, with the fire of infatuation; with birth, old age, death, sorrow, lamentation, misery, grief, and despair are they on fire. (*Mahāvagga*, I. 21.)[10]

The things of the world are on fire. They burn us because we become attached to them and want to possess them. Attachment and grasping *(taṇhā)* are responsible for producing those evil qualities *(kilesa)* of passion *(rāga)*, anger *(dosa)*, and delusion *(moha)*. Such evil qualities can be removed only by destroying attachment to the mirage-like world created by our misperception of things.

Freedom from attachment, in the Buddhist view, depends upon seeing the world as it really is—impermanent and in flux *(anicca)*, a continual process of arising and passing away. The conditioned nature of the world is succinctly described by the law of conditioned genesis *(paṭicca-samuppāda)*. In its simplest forms the law of conditioned genesis is stated as follows: "If this is, that comes to be; from the arising of this that arises" *(Saṁyutta-Nikāya*, II. 64). It is expanded in the following manner:

1. Through ignorance are conditioned volitional actions.
2. Through volitional actions is conditioned consciousness.
3. Through consciousness are conditioned mental and physical phenomena.
4. Through mental and physical phenomena are conditioned the six components of one's existence (i.e., the five physical sense organs and the mind).

5. Through the six components is conditioned the contact the mind and body have with the world.
6. Through this contact is conditioned sensation.
7. Through sensation are conditioned desire, thirst, and craving.
8. Through desire is conditioned clinging.
9. Through clinging is conditioned the very process of becoming (i.e., life through the cycles of re-existence).
10. Through the process of becoming is conditioned birth.
11. Through the process of birth are conditioned (12) decay, death, lamentation, pain, etc. . . .

The law of conditioned genesis tells us that nothing in the world exists independent of a web of conditioning factors. In short, the world we ordinarily perceive exists only in a qualified sense. Because the world of things is only a qualified reality, there is nothing within it deserving of ultimate worth and value. What is here today will be gone tomorrow; youth changes to age; beauty is transformed into ugliness; pleasure becomes pain; success turns into failure. Surely, the world of change *(anicca)* and of conditioned genesis *(paṭicca-samuppāda)* is but a "mass of suffering."

The above description has led some Western scholars to characterize Buddhism as world-denying. Such a characterization is unfair. In the Buddhist view the world defined by the senses is neither totally devoid of meaning and hence to be negated, nor is it affirmed as ultimately meaningful. The Buddhist view is a middle path. The mundane world is, indeed, the arena in which all of us live out our lives; however, given its conditioned, relative, and impermanent nature, being attached to its beauty, desiring to possess its rewards, and seeking its promises of happiness can only lead to disappointment, frustration, and despair. Only by seeking a higher end (Nirvāna) can the ultimately unsatisfactory nature of the sensate world be transcended. The Buddhist would agree with the Gospel writer that the mundane world is but a place where "moth and rust consume" and "thieves break in and steal." The world around us may be the place where the "drama of salvation is acted out," but salvation itself is not defined in the terms of the world.

## IMPERMANENCE AND ESCHATOLOGY

The New Testament description of the world from the perspective of its imminent and total transformation is clearly different from the Buddhist description in terms of impermanence *(anicca)* and conditioned genesis *(paṭiccasamuppāda)*. Yet, a common assumption underlies these differences, namely, that the things of this world have no lasting value. In the New Testament this viewpoint is tied to the conviction that Jesus Christ makes all things new, that time in relationship to Jesus has a fullness, meaning, and value that time measured in other terms does not. The latter time might be expressed in the words of the American playwright William Saroyan, as "minutes on a clock, but not time of living." Time of living for the Christian is "the fullness of time." It is not measurable in the usual sense of time measurement. It is totally or absolutely filled with meaning and value and, hence, not relative to any condition or qualification. Such "fullness of time" contrasts with "clock time" in which minute is relative to hour, hour to day, day to week, week to month until, as Saroyan puts it, life becomes dull, boring, meaningless, and empty.

I would suggest that the Buddhist description of meaningless time in terms of impermanence and conditionality can help deepen the Biblical insight into the passing nature of the goals and satisfactions of this world. Isaiah cried: "All flesh is grass, and all its beauty is like the flower of the field. . . . The grass withers, the flower fades; but the word of our God will stand for ever" (Isa. 40:6, 8). Matthew advised not to lay up "treasures on earth, where moth and rust consume and where thieves break in and steal." The crucifixion makes the obvious point that Jesus was not the Messiah who would restore the political and worldly fortunes of Israel but had ushered in a "kingdom not of this world," a kingdom brought about by the transformation of one's mind rather than by conformity to the norms and expectations of the world.

Such themes have emerged from time to time throughout Christian history. Sometimes they are connected with crisis periods in which the established norms and institutions of this world are in a state of radical flux. At other times non-Christian modes of thought have provided an idiom of understanding and expression peculiarly appropriate to a critical evaluation of the world. Yet such circumstances and influences are to be seen as the secondary rather than the primal cause of a particular attitude toward the world. Augustine, for example, was steeped in neo-Platonic thought; however, his confession, "I find no rest until I find my rest in thee," is a consequence of faith in a living God whose Truth surpasses all truth: "O Eternal Truth and True Love and Beloved Eternity! Thou art my God, to whom I sigh both night and day. When I first knew thee, thou didst lift me up, that I might see that there was something to be seen, though I was not yet fit to see it. . . . I realized that I was far away from thee in the land of unlikeness, as if I heard thy voice from on high: 'I am the food of strong men; grow and you shall feed on me; nor shall you change me, like the food of your flesh into yourself, but you shall be changed into my likeness.' "[11] Augustine's prayer did not mean a rejection of the world or the things of this world. Rather, the world of empirical facts is perceived to be neither wholly real nor wholly unreal. Insofar as it comes from God, i.e., the wholly real, it is real; but insofar as it does not, Augustine evaluates the empirical world as unreal.[12]

Although the theological framework of Theravāda Buddhism differs significantly from that of Second Isaiah, Matthew, and Augustine, all four share an analogous evaluation of the empirical, apparently real world relative to a higher reality. The Buddhist view of the world can enhance this perspective rooted in the eschatological setting in the Old Testament prophets and the New Testament Gospels and Epistles precisely because its interpretation is analogous but not the same. In particular the Buddhist interpretation emphasizes man's inveterate tendency to immortalize himself, to try to make permanent that which is transient, and eternal that which is temporal. It brings into high relief the Gospel writer's observation that mankind seems bent on trying to build castles on foundations of sand which inevitably collapse.

One might argue that the analogy drawn between Theravāda Buddhism and Christianity belies a considerable difference between their respective world views. Running through the Bible is the theme that the world is good because God created it and appointed man to help in its governance. In Buddhism the world is said to be unsatisfactory *(dukkha)*. Unfortunately, many Western commentators on Buddhism have not done justice to this Buddhist concept. The Buddhist does not, in fact, say that the world is inherently evil or suffering *(dukkha)*. Rather he claims that life is *dukkha* because we try to get something out of it that it does not have the capacity to grant. We expect the mundane and material world to provide us with lasting happiness and satisfaction. It cannot do so because of its evanescent nature. The worldly castles we build are, indeed, built on foundations of sand. Some may last longer than others; however, none can provide lasting meaning, value, peace, and happiness. To *expect* them to do so is an *illusion;* to be *disappointed* when they do not is to *suffer.*

The Buddhist makes a series of claims highly relevant to the chaotic world in which we live today, a world increasingly dominated by the quest for materialistic goals but at the same time satiated and dissatisfied by them. They are: (1) the true nature of the mundane and sensate world is its conditionality *(anicca, paṭicca-samuppāda),* (2) this conditioned world can only provide mankind with relative satisfaction, (3) man's highest goal is in relationship to but other than the conditioned world of relativity. These claims are valuable in and of themselves as part of the Theravāda Buddhist perspective on the world. However, they can also be used to enrich the Christian's orientation toward the world at a time when the eschatological perspective is becoming more and more timely. Buddhism can, in short, stimulate the Christian church to recapture its critical attitude toward the world, and also offer the Christian a thoughtful explanation for "being in the world but not of it."

As we have pointed out, there are strands in both the Old and New Testaments that offer a more critical and even hostile attitude toward the world than has been evidenced in much of the history of the Christian church in the modern period. Søren Kierkegaard's observation that Christendom in Denmark danced to the tune of "Merrily We Roll Along" fits the church in many parts of the world. By sympathetically encountering the Buddhist insight of the radically impermanent, continuously conditioned nature of the world, the Christian can be stimulated to restore this part of the meaning of the Biblical understanding of the world. There is no doubt that this perspective was weakened by the fact that the end-time did not come, that Paul's expectation of Jesus' imminent return was not realized. However, to reduce the New Testament's sense of living in the fullness of time to the literal reappearance of the Savior is to jeopardize the value of the Biblical critique of the world. We need to take seriously the Buddhist teaching that the fleeting reality of the world does not allow us to fashion God's kingdom on earth; that our worldly ambitions slip through our fingers as water passes through a sieve; that no structures or institutions of this world, including the church, can fill our lives with meaning and value. With this knowledge we can sit lightly to the world—or, in Buddhist terms, not be attached to it—in preparation for that complete fullness of time whose reality is personified in Jesus Christ.

Some readers may object that the argument of this chapter undermines the Bible's affirmation of the goodness of creation (e.g., Gen. 1:10) and God's love for his world (John 3:16). Of course, no one can deny the fact that the Biblical tradition depicts the world and human history as the arena where man encounters God. Yet the world and God, the wholly real in Augustine's terms, are not one and the same thing, and if one's primary loyalty is to the world on its own terms, then one fails to see the Truth and lives in unreality. Buddhism cogently reminds us that attachment to the world as it appears to our senses blinds us to the Truth.

A thought from The First Letter of John is pertinent: "Do not love the world or the things in the world. If any one loves the world, love for the Father is not in him. For all that is in the world, the lust of the flesh and the lust of the eyes and the pride of life, is not of the Father but is of the world. And the world passes away, and the lust of it; but he who does the will of God abides for ever" (I John 2:15–17).

Does this quotation remind you of an earlier passage quoted from a Buddhist text? Although the idiom and the symbolism differ, it is clearly reminiscent of the Buddha's testimony in the *Mahāvagga* (I. 21): "All things, O priests, are on fire. . . . The eye, O priests, is on fire; forms are on fire. . . ."

# Chapter 3

# It Is No Longer I Who Live

Dialogue of any kind begins when people have something of common interest to share with one another. Does this mean, then, that religious people can enter into dialogue simply because they share a common interest? Obviously such a consequence does not necessarily follow. Genuine dialogue emerges from shared experiences. As a result interreligious dialogue should begin with issues that people of different religious backgrounds have in common. If a Christian-Buddhist encounter began with the doctrine of God, it would likely focus on abstractions and remove the discussion from the level of common interest and concern. Questions of mere immediate relevance would be those which address the human situation as it is lived and then interpreted through the perspective of particular religious traditions. In short, interreligious dialogue becomes genuinely meaningful when it grows out of our common humanity; when we relate to each other not as a Christian, Buddhist, Hindu, or Muslim but as human beings whose sense of what it means to be human finds expression through our various faiths.

The way we perceive and relate to the world around us—the issue addressed in Chapter 2—and the question addressed here, What is the meaning of persons? are appropriate starting points for dialogue. In the following we shall first examine the Pauline notion of the self in terms of the Old Creation/New Creation polarity, then proceed to a brief analysis of the Theravāda Buddhist teaching of not-self *(an-attā)*, and conclude with a reconsideration of the conception of the new creation in the light of the not-self concept.

## OLD CREATION/NEW CREATION

"Therefore, if any one is in Christ, he is a new creation; the old has passed away, behold, the new has come." (II Cor. 5:17.) With these words Paul characterizes the fundamental movement of the Christian's life—from an old being under the power of the flesh to a new being in Christ. This movement from the Old to a New Creation underlies much of Paul's thought ranging from baptism to the resurrection. It must have reflected his own experience of having been reborn from an inauthentic existence to authentic existence by the power of the Christ event. He is convinced that the distinction between the New Creation in Christ and the Old Creation in Adam is as radically different as the gulf between life and death or non-being and being.

For Paul, the Old Creation is a profane existence dominated by three powers or forces: sin, flesh, and the law. As a result of bondage to them a person is not fully human, i.e., is alienated from his true nature. All three forces operate to prevent the realization of authentic existence. Each of them must be considered if we are to comprehend Paul's understanding of the Old Creation.

Sin, in Paul's eyes, is not primarily understood as acts, but as a power dominating one's action: "I can will what is right, but I cannot do it. For I do not do the good I want, but the evil I do not want is what I do. Now if I do what I do not want, it is no longer I that do it, but *sin which dwells within me*" (Rom. 7:18b–20, italics mine). Sin operates within us, crippling our best intentions and detouring us from our greatest good. Inauthentic existence submits to sin just as the world is cowed by evil powers and principalities. The individual, the church, and the world cannot escape this conflict between being and non-being. Paul experienced this tension within his own personal life to the extent that the outcome was predicated either as bondage to the flesh or as freedom in the spirit.

The flesh, for Paul, is the instrument of sin. In fact, it is so subservient to the power of sin that "wherever flesh is, all forms of sin are likewise present, and no good thing can live in the flesh."[1] The body of flesh epitomizes inauthentic existence: "Nothing good dwells within me, that is, in my flesh" (Rom. 7:18). The flesh cannot please God (Rom. 8:8) and those who set their minds on the flesh are dead to their true existence (Rom. 8:6). Flesh or the body of flesh refers to external, physical existence. It represents the outward side of life, the natural and the earthly; hence, anyone who is satisfied with the obvious, who boasts of his own worldly wisdom, who takes the satisfaction of the body to be an end in itself, who is content with the acclaim of the masses, who justifies himself according to tradition or any other external standard is in bondage to the flesh. The flesh is existence in unsanctified form because it cannot see beyond itself. It is life lived unto itself without reference to the ground of being. Those who live in the flesh, therefore, are literally in *bondage* to sin; those who delight in the pleasures of flesh will be *ruled* by the flesh; and those who take pride in the achievement of the law are necessarily *governed* by law.

The law, like the flesh and sin, characterizes the Old Creation because inevitably it seems to become an end in itself. In that manner the law acts as a power blinding a person to the highest reality beyond the law. When taken as an ultimate standard by which one judges his own righteousness, the law must be considered unrighteous. The law does not have the power to justify a person (Gal. 2:16) because to be justified is to be freed. By its very nature, however, the law restricts rather than frees. True, for Paul the Jewish law has a positive custodial function; but even accounting for the necessary role of law to maintain community, it is not essentially an agent of freedom but an agent of slavery. The law serves to bind a person to the external, to the flesh, to inauthentic existence. The powers ruling profane existence—sin, flesh, and the law—all lead one dominated by them into a condition of living death.

By way of contrast the powers that free a person from death to a new life are the Spirit and faith. In the new life or the New Creation the power of sin is broken by the power of God in Jesus Christ through the Spirit. The following examples point to some of the ways in which the Spirit dominates the New Creation just as sin dominated the Old: Christians are those who are led by the Spirit (Rom. 8:4); it is through the power of the Spirit that Christians are bound together in the body of the church (I Cor. 12:13); the Spirit endows a variety of gifts to members of the church (I Cor. 12:1); the fruits of the Spirit are love, joy, peace, patience, kindness, goodness, faithfulness, gentleness, and self-control (Gal. 5:22–23).

How does the Spirit effect authentic existence? It does so through faith. Faith is the necessary response to the activity of the Spirit. It is the act of self-emptying that enables one to be filled with the Spirit, the life power of the New Creation. Faith is a paradoxical glorying in weakness and suffering as a sign of new strength and power (II Cor. 11:21ff.). Faith is the giving up of the old so that the new can be received; it is the casting aside of sin, the flesh, and the law to be filled in return with a new being. The New Creation is a Spirit-dominated life designed by the power of God through the Spirit which makes all persons sons of God in the church, the body of Christ (Rom. 8:14f.).

The focus of the New Creation for Paul is being *in Christ.* He affirms this relationship for himself in such personal confessions as: "It is no longer I who live, but Christ who lives in me" (Gal. 2:20), or again in the third chapter of Philippians where he joyfully gives up all things that he "may gain Christ and be found in him" (Phil. 3:8–9). The centrality of this relationship is conveyed through various images in the Epistles. Those who are "in Christ" are "sons of God" through him; they are fellow "heirs" of the kingdom with Christ; they are the bride and Christ the husband (II Cor. 11:2). The Christian lives in the sacred when he has "clothed" himself in Christ (Rom. 13:14), and in all things the Christian is admonished to be an "imitator" of Jesus Christ (I Cor. 11:1). All these images bespeak the most intimate of relationships. They imply a unity of the individual with Christ but demand separateness as well, just as the image of the church as the body of Christ and the interworkings of the Spirit and faith demand both unity in the New Creation and yet the singularity of individual members.

As individuals, then, Christians are united in the one body. This one body is a New Creation, a new ontological reality established by the death and resurrection of Jesus Christ. To be "in Christ" is to participate in the Christ event. As Paul explains to the Corinthian Christians, "He died for all, that those who live might live no longer for themselves but for him who for their sake died and was raised" (II Cor. 5:15). Or again to the church at Rome: "Do you not know that all of us who have been baptized into Christ Jesus were baptized into his death? We were buried therefore with him by baptism into death, so that as Christ was raised from the dead by the glory of the Father, we too might walk in newness of life. For if we have been united with him in a death like his, we shall certainly be united with him in a resurrection like his. We know that our old self was crucified with him so that the sinful body might be destroyed, and we might no longer be enslaved to sin. For he who has died is freed from sin. But if we have died with Christ, we believe that we shall also live with him. For we know that Christ being raised from the dead will never die again; death no longer has dominion over him. The death he died he died to sin, once for all, but the life he lives he lives to God. So you also must consider yourselves dead to sin and alive to God in Christ Jesus" (Rom. 6:3–11).

Baptism for Paul means putting on Christ (Gal. 3:27), that

is, identifying with the central event of Jesus' life, his death and resurrection. For Paul, Jesus is the first of a new order of being, one who died to sin to be reborn to newness of life. Similarly, for the Christian, baptism denotes dying to an old life dominated by sin and putting on an entirely new life freed from bondage to world attachments. The new life is one established in God after the Jesus event, the perfect union of the human and the divine, the man who opened up new possibilities of existence for mankind.

The new self for Paul is one in which the old self or old personality has been completely changed. For this very reason the doctrine of the resurrection is central to Christianity. To be in Christ means to be radically transformed, not halfway changed or changed only in the mind or spirit. For Paul to be totally in Christ means, to use Buddhist terminology, that all five aggregates *(khandhas)* have undergone a transformation. For this reason Paul's discussion of the resurrection in I Cor., ch. 15, is coupled with his assertion that Jesus was the Second Adam, a new humanity. The old humanity, or the first Adam, lived by the flesh, and, hence, died according to the flesh. The new humanity after Jesus, the Second Adam, shares a new life so unlike the former that it can be likened only to immortality. Sin, the power dominating mortality, has now been conquered and Paul can exclaim: "Death is swallowed up in victory. . . . O death, where is thy sting? The sting of death is sin. . . . Thanks be to God, who gives us the victory through our Lord Jesus Christ" (I Cor. 15:54–57). Sin, the sting of death, has been removed by Jesus. He represents a new possibility of existence in which the old self is left behind and a new humanity achieved. For Paul this new life is found in Christ: "From now on . . . we regard no one from a human point of view; even though we once regarded Christ from a human point of view, we regard him thus no longer. Therefore, if any one is in Christ, he is a new creation; the old has passed away, behold, the new has come" (II Cor. 5:16–17).

## THE BUDDHIST CONCEPT
## OF NOT-SELF *(ANATTĀ)*

In Theravāda Buddhism the Pauline themes of the Old
Creation/New Creation find an analogy in the polarity of
self/not-self *(atta/anattā)*. The fact that Buddhism uses a
negative term *(an-atta)* to characterize the nature of selfhood has given rise to much misunderstanding. I once attempted to help a group of college students come to a deeper
understanding of the concept by arranging a month-long
meditation workshop. The purpose of the project was to introduce my students to an understanding of Buddhism
through the practice of Theravāda and Zen forms of meditation, by reading relevant meditation texts, and meeting to
discuss both their experiences in meditation and their reading. About thirty students were enrolled in the project,
which was being led by Chao Khun Sobhana Dhammasudhi,
a Thai monk from the Buddhapadīpa Temple in London, and
Rev. Eshin Nishimura, executive secretary of the Institute for
Zen Studies at Hanozono Buddhist University, Kyoto, Japan.
One afternoon's discussion stands out vividly in my mind.
The Chao Khun had been asking if the students' meditation
experience had deepened their understanding of the Buddhist notion of *anattā,* or not-self. Several confirmed that
meditation had given them much more insight into the Buddhist concept of person and personality. Approaching an understanding of not-self through the experience of meditation
led one participant to exclaim that this concept threatened
her security, and that she did not want to give up her "Western self." While she may not have understood the *anattā*
notion correctly, the challenge it provided was an important
part of the exercise. Certainly part of the intent of the not-
self teaching, especially when confronted through a meditation experience, is to call into question the nature of our
self-understanding. But what is the meaning of not-self in

Buddhist thought? Is it totally foreign to Western ways of thinking, or are there points of contact? In particular, how does the Buddhist view of personhood positively challenge the Christian view of personhood?

There are many references to the term *anattā* in the Pāli canonical materials of Theravāda Buddhism, although they have not always been interpreted in the same manner either by Buddhists or by Western scholars. For example, the famous admonition of the Buddha, "Be a lamp unto yourself," from the *Dhammapāda,* has been interpreted as implying a self *doctrine* rather than as an injunction to rely for salvation only upon oneself alone. Disagreements about the not-self teaching are aired in the *Kathāvatthu (Points of Controversy),* a textbook countering heretical teachings attributed to the Third Buddhist Council of the famous Indian monarch, Asoka (third century B.C.), in which the views of those who hold a doctrine of person *(puggalavāda)* are rejected. The classical Theravāda position is most often represented by the chariot simile taken from the dialogue between King Milinda (Menander) and Bhikkhu Nāgasena in the *Milindapañha (Questions of Milinda):*

> Then the venerable Nāgasena spoke to Milinda the king as follows:—
>
> "Your majesty, you are a delicate prince. . . , and if, your majesty, you walk in the middle of the day on hot sandy ground, and you tread on rough gravel, . . . your feet become sore, your body tired, the mind is oppressed, and the body-consciousness suffers. Pray, did you come afoot, or riding?"
>
> "Bhante [Reverend Sir], I do not go afoot: I came in a chariot."
>
> "Your majesty, if you came in a chariot, declare to me the chariot. Pray, your majesty, is the pole the chariot?"
>
> "Nay, verily, bhante."
>
> "Is the axle the chariot?"
>
> "Nay, verily, bhante."
>
> "Are the wheels the chariot?"

"Nay, verily, bhante."

"Is the chariot-body the chariot?"

"Nay, verily, bhante."

"Is the banner-staff the chariot?"

"Nay, verily, bhante. . . ."

"Pray, your majesty, are pole, axle, wheels, chariot-body, banner-staff, . . . unitedly the chariot?"

"Nay, verily, bhante."

"Is it, then, your majesty, something else besides pole, axle, wheels, chariot-body, banner-staff, . . . which is the chariot?"

"Nay, verily, bhante."

"Your majesty, although I question you very closely, I fail to discover any chariot. Verily now, your majesty, the word 'chariot' is a mere empty sound. . . ."

Then Milinda the king spoke to the venerable Nāgasena as follows:—

"Bhante Nāgasena, I speak no lie: the word 'chariot' is but a way of counting, term, appellation, convenient designation, and name for pole, axle, wheels, chariot-body, and banner-staff."

"Thoroughly well, your majesty, do you understand a chariot. In exactly the same way, your majesty, in respect of me, Nāgasena is but a way of counting, term, appellation, convenient designation, mere name for the hair of my head, hair of my body . . . brain of the head, form, sensation, perception, the predispositions, and consciousness. But in the absolute sense there is no Ego here to be found."[2]

What is it that the Buddhist not-self teaching denies? As Nāgasena puts it, there is no underlying self, no soul or substructure to the components of physical and mental life. Theravāda Buddhism devised several ways of analyzing the dual factors of the mental and physical coordinates of existence. The simplest and most famous is the list of five components or aggregates (body, sensations, perceptions, predispositions, consciousness) which appears in the *Milindapañha* and elsewhere in the Pāli canon. Another more naturalistic list is the thirty-two bodily parts beginning with the hair of the head, hair of the body, and so on. Later more scholastic analyses became more elaborate. All these methods of analyzing the components of human existence serve to make the same point—there is no *atta,* no Self, no Soul, no substructure to that collection of factors we call the "I" and the "You."

## THREE DIMENSIONS OF NOT-SELF

There are several important dimensions to this not-self doctrine in Buddhism. In the first place, it is integrated into the Buddha's particular path toward salvation. Preoccupation about the nature of the self can sidetrack one from the path toward the attainment of Nirvāna. Much like Søren Kierkegaard believed that the Hegelian philosophical system deceived a person about the ultimacy of the knowledge it provided, the Buddha believed that metaphysical questions did not tend toward edification. In the famous dialogue with Malunkyaputta, a follower of the Buddha desiring answers to such questions as to whether the world was eternal, the soul and body identical, or the saint existed after death, the Buddha replied in the following manner:

> "It is as if, Malunkyaputta, a man had been wounded by an arrow thickly smeared with poison, and his friends and companions, his relatives and kinsfolk, were to procure for him a physician or surgeon; and the sick man were to say, 'I will not have this arrow taken out until I have learned whether the man who wounded me belonged to the warrior caste, or to the Brahmin caste, or to the agricultural caste, or to the menial caste . . . (or) to what clan he belongs . . . (or) whether the man who wounded me was tall, or short, or of middle height . . . (or) whether the man who wounded me was black, or dusky, or of a yellow skin. . . .'
>
> "That man would die, Malunkyaputta, without ever having learned this.
>
> "In exactly the same way, Malunkyaputta, anyone who

should say, 'I will not lead the religious life under the Blessed One (the Buddha) until the Blessed One shall explain to me either that the world is eternal, or that the world is not eternal . . .';—that person would die, Malunkyaputta, before the Tathāgata had ever explained.

". . . Bear always in mind what it is that I have not explained, and what it is that I have explained. . . . I have not explained that the world is eternal . . . (or) not eternal; . . . that the world is finite . . . (or) infinite; . . . that the soul and the body are identical. . . . And why, Malunkyaputta, have I not explained this? Because . . . this profits not, nor has this to do with the fundamentals of religion, nor tends to aversion, absence of passion, cessation, quiescence, the supernatural faculties, supreme wisdom and Nirvāna. . . ." *(Majjhima-Nikāya, 63.)*[3]

The solution to a metaphysical problem may be intellectually interesting, but it can become an end in itself, thereby standing in the way of the solution of spiritual problems and the attainment of religious goals. Accordingly, the *anattā* teaching is neither an "eternalist" nor an "annihilationist" doctrine,[4] but a teaching which avoids the philosophical polemics of either position.

A second dimension of the not-self notion is its consistency with the Buddhist goal of non-attachment or Nirvāna. Logically speaking, how can selfishness, greed, ambition, lust, hatred, and similar qualities exist if the focal motivating point for such passions has been removed? Detachment and equanimity *(upekkhā),* the qualities of sainthood *(arahant),* arise through the practical elimination of ego-centeredness. An individual is able to act freed from the subjective biases, prejudices, and defenses or ego hang-ups only when he is totally aware of himself and his environment. Such total awareness is tantamount, in the Buddhist view, to the elimination of the ego *(anattā),* an artificial construct produced through ignorance *(avijjā)* and sensory attachment *(kilesa).* The psychological and moral goal of Buddhism, i.e., *upek-*

*khā,* as well as the state of being denoted by that goal, i.e., Nirvāna, is, therefore, thoroughly consistent with the Buddhist teaching of not-self *(anattā).*

The third dimension of the not-self doctrine is the most difficult to discuss but the most rewarding for the enterprise of interreligious dialogue. If the Buddhist position of not-self, or *anattā,* is a rejection of the concept of *atta,* a substantive self or soul, then the Buddhist goal obviously cannot be the attainment of an eternal soul or self. The goal cannot be depicted as a movement from *anattā,* an objectionable state, to *atta,* a desirable state. Rather, the state of not-self *(anattā)* denotes the way things really are—devoid of essential substance or soul. As a result, the realization of the *anattā,* or not-self, character of life is part of the Buddhist's aim. In the Buddhist analysis of existence, ordinary people conceive of themselves in terms of some kind of self, soul, or ego *(atta),* and in turn, this conception motivates much of their action. *Anattā* represents a different state of being characterized by *upekkhā,* non-ego or non-self motivated action. Such a state of being is designated by the term *nirvāna,* which means having the passions "blown out" or being a not-self. *Anattā,* on the basis of such an analysis, represents a transformed state of existence. One is changed into such an entirely different person that the only way he can be designated is by a negation—a not-self *(an-atta).* The springs of action have been so radically altered that the ordinary categories describing action in the world no longer apply. The completely realized man, therefore, is totally emptied *(suññatā),* a not-self by the ordinary standards of selfhood.

Within the Buddhist tradition the not-self, or *anattā,* interpretation of persons runs into several problems. If there is no self, what is the bearer of moral responsibility, what is reborn through the cycles of lifetimes, what attains salvation *(nirvāna)?* Such questions lay at the root of several key doctrinal controversies within Indian Buddhism. We have already mentioned that the Third Buddhist Council rejected the position of the *puggalavādins,* those who held there was a "person," a locus of continuity sufficient to answer the kinds of questions mentioned above. Other Buddhist schools went even further, postulating a universal, true Self or Buddha nature. Generally speaking, then, we find a tension between those schools of Buddhism which reject a substantive concept of the self, and those who do not. Yet, as the Buddha clearly perceived, such doctrinal or philosophical disputes run the risk of beclouding the main religious issue. They can sidetrack the spiritual quest for a higher mode of self-realization. The not-self *(anattā)* teaching, therefore, does not engage the philosophical debate of annihilationism and eternalism. It does not propose a *doctrine* of personhood at all but points the mind toward a higher stage of spiritual life. In a similar manner the chariot metaphor or simile is not meant to be an *argument* from analogy for a particular view of the self, but rather a suggestion, a provocation of the mind, a stimulus to reflection beyond ordinary definitions or limits of what it means to be a person.

## THE NEW CREATION
## IN THE LIGHT OF ANATTĀ

We have seen how the Buddhist teaching of not-self *(anattā)* is part of a meaning complex consistent with such terms as equanimity *(upekkhā),* the supreme goal of dispassion and emptiness *(suññatā).* That is, not-self denotes a new state of existence or level of being which contrasts with an old life of grasping *(taṇhā),* sensory attachment *(kilesa),* passion *(lobha),* delusion *(moha),* and hatred *(dosa).* Other distinctions made between these two types of existence are darkness and ignorance *(avijjā)* versus light and knowledge *(vijja),* and bondage *(bandhana)* versus freedom *(mutti).*

Seen from such a perspective, the meaning inherent in not-self closely resembles the meaning in Paul's notion of the New Creation in Christ. We have seen how Paul contrasts two types of creation, states of being, or existence. The old life is one of bondage to the flesh, dominated by sin and necessarily regulated by law. The new life is a life of faith filled with the power of God (i.e., the Holy Spirit) and freed from the conditions of existence characterized by the old Adam or old mankind. From this description we can see a basic similarity in the movement of the religious life from a deprived state of being to a fulfilled one despite the differences in language and symbol between the two traditions.

Beyond this similar structure of the Old Creation/New Creation, however, the Buddhist understanding of man as *anattā*, or not-self, can help the Christian more fully appreciate what has usually been interpreted as the Christian virtue of selflessness. We often encounter this teaching in the Gospels. The follower of Jesus is admonished to forgive not seven times but seventy times seven (Matt. 18:22), to turn the other cheek instead of following the usual law of retribution of an eye for an eye and a tooth for a tooth (Matt. 5:38), and to take up the cross and follow Jesus (Matt. 10:38). Such admonitions do, indeed, have an ethical import; however, beyond the change in manner of behavior there resides a change of character or being. The cross, itself, symbolizes this change. It is the supreme example of *kenōsis,* or self-emptying: it is man totally emptying himself to be God; it is man dying to conquer mortality in order to be reborn to immortality. The Christian takes up the same cross of self-emptying. In Paul's terms he dies the death of Jesus in order to share in the life of the resurrection.

The Buddhist teaching of not-self can help the Christian penetrate beyond the merely ethical meaning of the Christian teaching of selflessness. To be selfless in act means to act without regard to self, to have transcended the defenses of the ego which inhibit acting altruistically, to give of one's self as an automatic reflex. Such a mode of being involves a radical revolution that can be no less than a cutting off of an old life, and the adoption of a new one, or a death and a rebirth.

The death event is the most crucial, for there can be no totally new being unless the old one is given up. For this reason the not-self teaching is the focal point of Theravāda Buddhism, just as the crucifixion is the focal event in the life of Jesus. In Buddhism *anattā* has both its negative and positive components. That is, on the one hand, it points to the displacement of the self-center; on the other, however, it denotes a new life of non-attachment and equanimity. For the Christian the crucifixion is but one side of the climax of the Christ event; the other side is the resurrection. The one implies the other but it must be borne in mind that the crucifixion is prior. Without the crucifixion, there can be no resurrection; without self-emptying there can be no human fulfillment; without death there can be no new life.

The Buddhist concept of not-self focuses our attention on the uncompromising nature of the New Creation. In Buddhism to see one's true nature necessarily means to have "naughted" all other contingent and erroneous self-images. In short, authentic personhood transcends all personae. The New Creation represents a similar authenticity, or, if you will, divineness. In the language of Meister Eckhart, "to be full of things is to be empty of God, while to be empty of things is to be full of God."[5] How full of "things" most of us are—projections for the future, worries about the past, bound by our plans, limited by our definitions, unable truly to be in the present.

The Christian who truly penetrates the meaning of the not-self *(anattā)* teaching may rediscover the deepest meaning of the spiritual journey from the Old to the New Creation. Furthermore, he will come to see the life of Christ as one where the old self-image has been crucified so that a new being in the likeness of God might emerge.

# Chapter 4

# True Righteousness

Sometime ago a well-known abbot of a monastery in Chiang Mai, Thailand, and I were discussing Buddhism and Christianity. At one point in the conversation the Venerable Abbot said: "From everything I have read it appears that all Christianity requires of its adherents is faith in Jesus Christ. That seems inadequate. In Buddhism moral virtue *(sīla)* and contemplative practices or mental cultivation *(samādhi)* are stages on the path to wisdom *(paññā)*, a higher righteousness. Buddhism seems to me to be both more comprehensive and realistic!"

In reply I pointed out that whereas faith was certainly the focus of the Christian notion of righteousness, Christianity also prized moral virtue and good works, and many Christian thinkers wrote about spiritual progress. Yet the abbot's point was well taken. The line from Paul through Augustine, Martin Luther, Søren Kierkegaard, and Karl Barth has tended to create a dichotomy between faith on the one hand and good works according to the law on the other: "For we hold that a man is justified by faith apart from works of law" (Rom. 3:28); "Now it is evident that no man is justified before God by the law; for 'He who through faith is righteous shall live'" (Gal. 3:11). For Paul, righteousness before God cannot be earned. It is not *achieved* but is a concomitant of the new life in Christ. Hence, faith in the sense of trust and obedience rather than works is ascribed as true righteousness. Indeed, for Paul, it seems that works righteousness is antithetical to faith, just as the Old Creation is the antithesis of the New Creation.

At the outset we are required at least to acknowledge the complexity of Christian thought on this issue. For example, the Thomistic tradition upholds the moral and intellectual virtues as well as the theological ones. It sees natural and human law in an essential teleological relationship to eternal law. Nevertheless, the Christian concept of righteousness has been troubled over the years by the apparent conflict between faith and works, or the law and the gospel. In this chapter we do not propose to explore this problem in depth, but, rather, to develop briefly the Pauline line suggested above; then to examine one or two ways in which Buddhism addresses the concept of righteousness; and finally, in the light of that discussion, to suggest a reconsideration of the place of good works in the scheme of true righteousness.


## FAITH AND WORKS

What constitutes righteousness in Paul's thought? Quite clearly righteousness cannot be limited to works of the law. On the contrary, the law becomes sin precisely at the point the individual defines his own righteousness in terms of it. Why should this be the case? Because at the moment of self-justification one stands alienated from a greater possibility, God's power, truth, and love. Righteousness in its most fundamental Pauline sense, then, means to be put into a right relationship with God in the sense of being reconciled to God, the source of new life. This is not something man deserves or can earn. It is a gift of God's grace. The righteousness of God is reckoned the righteousness of faith, and the righteousness of faith is a hoped-for possibility seemingly beyond human probability (Rom. 4:13-20). Therefore, one is justified, one becomes righteous, redeemed and sanctified, affirmed and made whole by the ultimate paradox—life out

of death. The Christ event as life out of death is the fulfillment of the law by grace. For Paul, obedience to the law and
faith in God's grace represent two different modes of being:
"But now we have been released from the law, having died
to that which held us imprisoned, in order to serve in the new
life of the Spirit" (Rom. 7:6).

Paul's concept of true righteousness cannot be divorced
from his polemic against the Jewish law which found formu-
lation in his doctrine of justification by faith. This polemic is
not directed against the law as such, but the use of the law
to achieve righteousness. While in the ultimate sense life
lived by the Spirit or by the power of God manifested in the
Christ event transcends the law, for Paul the law is more than
merely the agent of sin. Paul refers to it as the law of God
(Rom. 7:22), and as such it bears witness to God's purposes
and demands. The law also performs the important function
of showing sin to be sin (Rom. 7:11–13), and "holds men in
custody" (Gal. 3:23) prior to the Christ event. From the perspective of faith, therefore, we can say that the law is an
instrument of God. Christ is the end *(telos)* of the law in the
paradoxical sense that he "ends" the law as a way to salvation
and is also the fulfillment of the law. In short, for Paul, the
law is totally subsumed under the *telos* of a higher righteousness.

Paul's suspicion of works righteousness has been shared by
Augustine, Luther, Kierkegaard, and Barth. Their solutions
to the faith/works bipolarity are not the same, of course, for
their contexts differed. However, it is worth noting that, like
Paul, each saw the problem in polemical terms. For Augustine it was the Pelagian compromise of God's grace, for Luther the works-righteousness abuses of the Roman Church,
for Kierkegaard the meaningless, institutional Christianity of
the Church of Denmark, and for Barth the bankruptcy of
Protestant liberalism in the post-World War II era.

For Augustine, the most important of the early Western
church fathers, Pelagius compromised the gospel by making

it into a moral system men are capable of fulfilling through free will, reason, and conscience endowed in all men by God's grace. Both the law and the gospel work together to encourage men to the right use of the light they have already been given. Hence, Augustine sees Pelagius compromising the distinction between life lived under the law and under grace. Although his early strongly polemical anti-Pelagian writings are softened in his later, mature thought, even there he sees good works as a product of God's grace: "Justification is grace simply and entirely. . . . We [must] understand that even those good works of ours which are recompensed with eternal life, belong to the grace of God, because of what is said by the Lord Jesus: 'Without me ye can do nothing.' "[1]

Martin Luther, the father of the sixteenth-century German Reformation, in his commentary on Galatians distinguishes the moral law as a creation of man's reason from true righteousness which comes by faith alone. And in his even more famous *Treatise on Christian Liberty* he pens: "A Christian man is free from all things and over all things, so that he needs no works to make him righteous and to save him, since faith alone confers all these things abundantly. But should he grow so foolish as to presume to become righteous, free, saved, and a Christian by means of some good work, he would on the instant lose faith and all its benefits; a foolishness aptly illustrated in the fable of the dog who runs along a stream with a piece of meat in his mouth, and, deceived by the reflection of the meat in the water, opens his mouth to snap at it, and so loses both the meat and the reflection."[2]

In the nineteenth century the Danish theologian and church critic, Søren Kierkegaard, was also much moved by the Pauline tradition of salvation by faith alone. His model of faith, as for Paul, was Abraham, whom Kierkegaard referred to as a knight of faith. The knight of faith stands in an absolute relationship to God uncompromised by any lesser commitments. He acts according to a higher end which seemingly contradicts the laws of men, e.g., Abraham's belief in God's promise despite its absurdity from a human perspective. To this religious man, Kierkegaard contrasted the ethical man who justifies himself according to law, and the aesthete who lives to satisfy his pleasures. These earlier "stages on life's way" are not stepping-stones to a higher end, but rather are obstructions to it. Kierkegaard dramatizes the nature of faith by use of the analogy of a swimmer alone over forty thousand fathoms of water who, having despaired of any conceivable means of rescue, is miraculously saved. True righteousness, then, is faith—the complete giving up of oneself as a necessary and sufficient condition for an absolute relationship with God.

The notion of true righteousness through faith alone and not works has been a prevailing strand in Christian thought. This perspective intends to formulate a moral posture that defines a state of being wholly other than that represented by those who justify themselves by the consequences of their actions. It is assumed by both Paul and Luther that a man of faith will do good works; however, good works follow as a necessary consequence of one whose will has been transformed. One who is no longer will-ful will, perforce, act in accord with that change. Little attention is given to the preparation for this change, or the role of ethics in relationship to the new being. While other views, such as the Thomistic, provide more latitude for natural and human virtues, even they are fulfilled only by the theological virtues. Thomas places a higher value on natural and human law than Paul because human reason has natural principles impressed on it by God. However, for both Paul and Thomas the locus of true righteousness is a higher, divine *Telos*. For Paul, the law's positive functions are evaluated from the perspective of men's justification by God in Christ; for Thomas, the moral law is part of the divine wisdom which directs all things to the attainment of their true ends.

## KARMA AND GOOD WORKS

How does Buddhism stand on the issues implicit in the Pauline notion of true righteousness? In the previous chapters we have argued that dialogue with Buddhism has the potential for helping us reassess the meaning of particular focuses of the Biblical faith. Now we propose that the Buddhist justification of moral righteousness can function to augment the traditional Pauline treatment of the works of the law without threatening his interpretation of the righteousness of the new being in Christ.

"By their deeds ye shall know them." This terse saying from the West has much in common with the Buddhist understanding of *karma*. In its most general usage, *karma* simply refers to any action. In Buddhism and several other Indian religious traditions, action came to be invested with a causative power extending beyond an immediate, pragmatic effect. An act produces a visible result, e.g., teasing a friend makes him angry, but a less visible result is the effect it produces on us. Every action we perform has both external and internal consequences. The external consequences are often, though not necessarily, measurable or quantifiable. The internal consequences, that is, the effect of our actions on our character and our psychological and physiological well-being, are less evident. In both cases, however, our actions are not neutral. They produce an effect either for good or for ill. The Buddhist is particularly concerned about the internal effects of *karma*. One's *karma*, or character, affects one's total well-being in this life as well as the next. To act for good is to produce good; to act for evil is to produce evil:

> Let any one who holds self dear,
> That self keep free from wickedness;
> For happiness can ne'er be found
> By any one of evil deeds.

Assailed by death, in life's last throes,
At quitting of this human state,
What is it one can call his own?
What with him take as he goes hence?
What is it follows after him,
And like a shadow ne'er departs?

His good deeds and his wickedness,
Whate'er a mortal does while here;
'T is this that he can call his own,
This with him take as he goes hence.
This is what follows after him,
And like a shadow ne'er departs.

Let all, then, noble deeds perform,
A treasure-store for future weal;
For merit gained this life within,
Will yield a blessing in the next.
                    (*Saṁyutta-Nikāya*, III. i. 4.)[3]

Every act, good or bad, produces a corresponding good or bad effect. These effects *(vipāka)* have a causative force, calculable either *ad seriatim* or cumulatively depending on the interpreter, which conditions the individual's well-being in the present as well as the future. In practice most contemporary Theravāda Buddhists perceive the conditioning power of *karma* in terms of religiously meritorious good deeds such as giving donations to a temple, providing food for the monks on morning alms rounds, and so on, rather than ethically meritorious good deeds such as keeping the five precepts (e.g., not to kill, steal, lie, etc.), or helping those in need. The latter is karmically wholesome, to be sure, but "doing merit" is calculated primarily in terms of action benefiting the Buddhist monkhood. It should be noted that in contemporary Buddhist practice in Southeast Asia a broadening of the range of religiously meritorious acts is taking place. Due largely to the impact of training programs in community and rural development, projects such as the building of new roads, sanitary wells, and classrooms under the encouragement of the Buddhist monastic order are perceived as religiously meritorious acts. Thus acts performed that are not of direct benefit to the order are now being interpreted as "doing merit."

The practice of emphasizing external, religious acts which we witness in Theravāda Buddhist countries today is not entirely faithful to the scriptural tradition of Theravāda Buddhism. While the act itself is important, especially the good ethical act, the intention is even more so:

> When a man's deeds are performed through covetousness, arise from covetousness, are occasioned by covetousness, originate through covetousness, wherever his personality may be, there these deeds ripen, and wherever they ripen, there he experiences the fruition of those deeds, be it in the present life or some subsequent one; when a man's deeds are performed through hatred ... (or) are performed through infatuation, arise from infatuation, are occasioned by infatuation, originate in infatuation, wherever his personality may be, there these deeds ripen, and wherever they ripen, there he experiences the fruition of these deeds, be it in the present life, or in some subsequent one.
>
> These, O Bhikkhus, are the three conditions under which deeds are produced. (Aṅguttara-Nikāya, iii. 33.)[4]

The text goes on to say that if covetousness, hatred, and infatuation are rooted out, then the resultant *deeds* are "abandoned, uprooted, pulled out of the ground like a palmyra tree, and become non-existent and not liable to spring up again in the future."

Because in the early Theravāda tradition the act's intention or motivation was so crucial, the ethics of good deeds were directly related to the acquisition of right intentions and right intentions were a product of mental training. Thus, the *Dhammapāda*, Buddhism's most famous text, begins with the twin verses:

> All that we are is the result of what we have thought; it is founded on our thoughts, it is made up of our thoughts. If a man speaks or acts with an evil thought, pain follows him, as

the wheel follows the foot of the ox that draws the carriage.

All that we are is the result of what we have thought; it is founded on our thoughts, it is made up of our thoughts. If a man speaks or acts with a pure thought, happiness follows him, like a shadow that never leaves him.[5]

In Buddhism we see a direct connection between the mind and mental training and outward behavior and action.

On the level of the ordinary person in the daily traffic of the mundane world the law of *karma* is the most operative force in the realm of behavior. It strongly emphasizes individual moral responsibility in terms of intention, act, and consequence. In the opinion of some interpreters the law of *karma* together with *saṁsāra,* or the doctrine of rebirth, offers not only a plan to explain behavior and status but a strong rationale for the performance of good deeds. Despite the normative significance of *karma* in the relative world of human affairs, however, the final aim of the Buddhist is to achieve a state of being where deeds are no longer conditioning; where action is no longer calculated in terms of merit and demerit; in short, where one has overcome the ordinary distinctions between good and evil. Such a state of being is denoted by the term *nirvāna.* It is the state of the *arahant,* the saint who has become so transformed that he is no longer subject to the power of *karma* and *saṁsāra. Karma,* therefore, operates in the relative or conditioned sphere, but not in the unconditioned sphere.

Buddhism has been characterized as a Middle Way between the practical extremes of indulgence on the one hand and asceticism on the other. Buddhism as a path or a way not only points to a higher goal, or *summum bonum,* but proposes to encompass all aspects of life. In this regard Buddhism does not differ from the other great historic religions which are holistic in their teachings. The most-oft-cited paradigm of the Buddhist Middle Way is the Noble Eightfold Path —(1) Right Speech, Action, and Livelihood; (2) Right Effort,

Mindfulness, and Concentration; and (3) Right Understanding and Thought—structured in terms of: (1) good works/ moral virtue *(sīla)*, (2) mental cultivation and concentration *(samādhi)*, and (3) saving knowledge or wisdom *(paññā)*. On the one hand, the path is progressive, moving from the development of moral and ethical virtues to the training of the mind and the attainment of wisdom and self-perfection. On the other hand, any one stage of the path also presupposes the other two, so that, for example, the person of true wisdom also cultivates the mind and is truly righteous.

The Buddhist Middle Way can also be interpreted in terms of the dual concepts of *karma* and Nirvāna.[6] The ultimate goal of Nirvāna presupposes self-perfection or the realization of a not-self state of being (see Chapter 2). Although ultimately all aspects of the Buddhist way are seen in terms of the highest goal which stands for a completely transformed state of being, the Middle Way nature of Buddhism also means that the significance of proximate or karmic goals also cannot be denied. To live according to the operation of *karma* cannot be avoided until one reaches Nirvāna, as karmic justice is as inexorable as God's law. Furthermore, to strive to better oneself karmically offers a reward in and of itself, but it also anticipates the possibility of gradual perfection until—lifetimes from now—Nirvāna can be realized. In short, the operations of *karma* and karmic ethics, if we may call them that, constitute both an independent realm of moral activity and an interrelated part of the way to Nirvāna. *Karma* and Nirvāna, therefore, have an ambivalent relationship to each other. *Karma* functions independently to define the nature of proximate goals and activity and their consequences for good or evil, yet looks forward to a higher righteousness where its own power is negated. In the following section we will suggest that this two-tiered system, particularly the karmic interpretation of activity, has a special relevance for a reconsideration of Christian righteousness.

## KARMA AND CHRISTIANITY

Winston L. King argues in his provocative book, *Buddhism and Christianity, Some Bridges of Understanding,* that *karma* as a supreme moral agent can be related to the Christian concept of God as ground of the moral order. *Karma* as moral order does, indeed, have similarities with Christianity on this metaphysical level; moreover, the emphasis on individual moral responsibility and the distinction between karmic and nirvanic ethics provide particularly suggestive perspectives for interreligious dialogue.

The period of rapid transition in which we find ourselves today has had vast consequences for modes of social organization and behavior. In the West the breakdown of traditional family structures, serious challenges to governmental authority, and the rise of various anti-establishment movements are all signs of the strains within traditional forms of social and political organization. There have been accompanying responses in value orientations and modes of behavior considered virtuous in times past to revolutionary substitutes defying what has been considered acceptable behavior by dominant majorities. The result has been an ethical and moral disruption causing consternation among many, and among some a serious quest for new norms and forms of behavior more viable to a world in crisis. Such a fluctuating situation provides an opportunity for Western Christians to look seriously at non-Western and non-Christian ethical forms for help in facing the dilemmas of the present time. Several aspects of the Buddhist teaching of *karma* can, I believe, be of benefit. They include the two I have mentioned—the strong stress on individual moral responsibility and the distinction between what we shall call karmic and nirvanic ethics.

The distinction between karmic and nirvanic ethics engenders karmic action with a causative force in terms of proximate or relative goals but not in terms of ultimate goals. While acts abstained from on the basis of infatuation, hatred, and delusion may produce beneficial results, they do not cause or bring about Nirvāna. Nirvāna is not caused by merit or, in Christian terms, salvation is not gained by good works. Such a distinction between karmic and nirvanic goals can help the Christian to re-appreciate the role of the law or normative ethics in relationship to faith. Neither Jesus nor Paul rejected the law. The Gospels tell us that Jesus came to fulfill the law (Matt. 5:17), and we have seen how, for Paul, the law had an intermediate role prior to becoming a new being in Christ. From a Buddhist perspective, we might say that every act in the world of the law, i.e., the relative world, has a consequence for good or for ill and that this law is inexorable. It is the supreme operative principle in the world in which most of us live. Only the saints, the sons of God, those who have been created anew in Christ, are exempted from it. They have transcended the ordinary distinctions between good and evil as defined by the law and the causative effect of *karma;* therefore, they cannot be governed by the law or by *karma.* Such a distinction between the ethics of the Old Creation (karmic ethics) and the ethics of the New Creation (nirvanic ethics) allows the Christian to retain the radical claim of salvation by faith alone without compromising a rationale for taking seriously the inexorable consequences of acts performed in the mundane world. For Paul those outside of faith are under the law. In Buddhist terms we would say that until the attainment of perfect equanimity one is subject to the karmic law of moral act and consequence. This last point brings into sharp relief the key significance of moral responsibility in terms of cause and effect. We shall close this section with a discussion of this issue.

Highlighted by ecological and population concerns, affluent, technologically advanced nations are beginning to realize the truth of the law of *karma*— that every act has a consequence for good or evil. Until quite recently the evolutionary myth of things getting better and better in every way dominated the technological mentality. Industrial progress was accepted as an *a priori* good and it was thought that nature could provide an inexhaustible supply of resources to feed this progress. As a result, in the name of progress and industrialization some natural resources are being threatened with depletion; living space is being seriously defaced; and the very air we breathe and water we drink has become poisoned to a greater or lesser extent. Scientists such as Paul Ehrlich at the University of California have looked at the problems of population and pollution, and have made grim prophecies about the future of mankind on the earth if radical changes are not made.

One way the Christian can address these and numerous other problems facing modern societies ranging from urban rehabilitation to rising crime rates and drug addiction is to develop a rationale for individual moral responsibility utilizing insights from the law of *karma.* An act cannot be isolated from its intention or its consequence. In particular we cannot act without experiencing the result in our own lifetime. We are the consequence of what we have done and intend to do, a composite of inheritance, present conditioning, and future projection. The actor is not isolated from the act. Rather, the act and actor, the thought and the thinker, are but extensions of each other. Western behavioral psychology has tended to emphasize the effect of external conditioning on the individual. For example, psychosis may be attributed to childhood rearing patterns, urban crime to ghetto environment, youthful violence to the influence of television, etc. While such a psychological perspective is helpful in understanding and correcting undesirable behavior, it tends to place the responsibility for action on forces outside the individual. From the karmic perspective environment and individual are part of a mutually conditioned/conditioning complex. Act and thought are seen not so much as the product of a conditioning environment, but as conditioning agencies themselves.

In short, karmic morality stresses the central role we play in shaping what we become. It emphasizes the fact that we can rise above our environment, and, eventually, become freed from the bonds of habituation that, to a large degree, we have created for ourselves. From the perspective of karmic ethics normative patterns are not created by external forces, but are patterns of our own making. Through a thorough understanding of the consequential nature of thought and action, karmic ethics can help the Christian devise an ethical program appropriate to his contemporary world without jeopardizing the fundamental insight behind the position of salvation by faith and not works righteousness.

## A HIGHER RIGHTEOUSNESS

We have taken the position that the Buddhist understanding of *karma* offers a timely perspective on the way Christians might justify good works without undermining the integrity of the notion of a higher righteousness rooted in the concepts of faith and grace. Now I would like to return to the conversation with the Chiang Mai abbot who asserted that in Buddhism no conflict exists between various stages on the Buddhist path and a seemingly transcendental state of higher righteousness represented by Nirvāna. This assertion raises the question of whether Buddhism can contribute to the Christian understanding of true righteousness itself as well as offer a way of justifying relevant moral and ethical patterns of a more proximate nature.

The Buddhist notion of religion as a path or a way has the virtue of reminding us that our faith does not exist in isolation from the rest of life. Our faith is the way we are going, the way we are living. Hence, like any undertaking it demands planning and systematic effort. Unfortunately, so much of the planning and effort we put into our faith seems directed less to our spiritual well-being or a higher righteousness and more to the well-being of the church as an institution. Paul's metaphor of the athlete is relevant here. The athlete trains himself systematically to master certain skills, and to attain a high degree of physical and mental adeptness in his particular sport. In Chapter 5 we shall focus on the spiritual disciplines which are part of the Buddhist "training." Here, however, our point is a more general one. Our religion is an enterprise affecting all aspects of our life. It is not merely an institution, a body of creeds and confessions, a series of well-intended committee meetings, and so on. Yet, do we prepare ourselves to walk the way of faith? Are we "in shape" spiritually to bear the yoke of the new being in Christ? Or does such a question itself raise the issue of works righteousness in our own minds as we read it? I would venture to say that for many of us it does, and precisely for this reason the question is worth considering. The ingrained dichotomy in much of Protestant Christianity between works and faith has engendered a suspicion of the notion of religion as a Way. Buddhism maintains that religion is a Way and yet does not relativize or compromise its final goal (Nirvāna). Good works in this sense prepare us for the Truth. In and of themselves they are not the Truth. I would suggest that theologically faith and works are not necessarily contradictory but are only necessarily bipolar. Works are not faith, but as part of the Way works are a necessary but not sufficient condition for true righteousness just as in Buddhism moral virtue (sīla) is perceived as the foundation of mental cultivation and saving knowledge.

Finally, does the Buddhist understanding of true righteousness provoke the Christian to reevaluate the life of faith? Perhaps the abbot is right—for most of us faith is too simple. It is an easy way out—"Have faith and do what you will." A Buddhist perspective would rather uphold the perspective of "Faith seeking Understanding." Faith is, indeed, simple, but in the sense of profundity rather than easy to understand. Understanding comes as a result of walking the Way. It is objective, detached, insightful. Faith and understanding cannot be separated any more than the Way and the Goal. Too often, perhaps, Christians place faith and understanding at odds in the same manner that we dichotomize faith and works. True righteousness in Buddhism denotes a state of being righted; to be righted is to see rightly or to have understanding. To have the wisdom of understanding means one has walked the Way. Perhaps the abbot is right; perhaps our faith is "too small."

# Chapter 5

# Freedom Now!

"Freedom now! Freedom now!" The chant of "Freedom now!" still reverberates around the world. It comes from the lips of the black majority in South Africa and Rhodesia, from Palestinian refugees in the Middle East, and from Muslim rebels in the Philippines. The United States said that it fought the Indochina war to free South Vietnam to determine its own political future, and the North Vietnamese claimed that they fought it to liberate their brothers from colonial imperialism. Freedom is one of the most cherished yet least understood ideals in the world today. It also has been and continues to be at the center of the Buddhist and Christian religious traditions. The Buddhist ideal of freedom and the way to its realization, seemingly so different from the Christian, reside at the very core of the dialogue between these two traditions. We shall first look at the Christian concept of freedom before turning to the Buddhist concepts of liberation and path.

## CHRISTIAN FREEDOM

"Know the truth, and the truth will make you free." (John 8:32.) The Christian as well as the Buddhist aims at the attainment of freedom. A new resurrection life of freedom is contrasted to an old life bound by sin. For Luther freedom was the hallmark of the Christian life, and Kierkegaard contrasted the freedom of the knight of faith with the individual bound to justify himself by the law. For both Luther and Kierkegaard the true Christian life cannot be earned by fulfilling the law. It is above the measurable categories of the law and can only come about as a consequence of a total transformation beyond the capacity of an individual to achieve for himself. Thus, the individual is freed from self-striving and self-justification. He can only empty himself in faith and be born again by the grace and power of God, the very ground of being itself.

The first theologian of Christian freedom was the apostle Paul. He prized freedom as a gift of the New Creation in Christ. The person who has died to the old self is freed from the power of sin dominating it (Rom. 6:7): "The law of the Spirit of life in Christ Jesus has set me free from the law of sin and death" (Rom. 8:2). Christian freedom is freedom from those powers dominating mundane existence, the powers represented by the flesh, sin, and mortality. Paul felt his earlier life to be so dominated by them that he was led to write to the church at Rome: "I do not do the good I want, but the evil I do not want is what I do. Now if I do what I do not want, it is no longer I that do it, but sin which dwells within me" (Rom. 7:19–20). The old life of mortality, finiteness or of fleshly existence is both limited (i.e., ends in death) and bound (i.e., governed by sin). The new life in Christ is unlimited (i.e., death has been swallowed up, mortality has been conquered by immortality, the fleshly body becomes a resurrection body) and free (i.e., the power of sin has been conquered and replaced by the power of God).

Freedom does not mean the license to do what one wants. Luther insisted that the Christian in his freedom was at the same time the lord of all and the servant of all: "A Christian man is a perfectly free lord of all, subject to none. A Christian man is a perfectly dutiful servant of all, subject to all. Although these two theses seem to contradict each other . . . they are Paul's own, who says, in I Corinthians 9, 'Whereas I was free, I made myself servant of all,' and Romans 8, 'Owe no man anything but to love one another.' Now love by its very nature is ready to serve and to be subject to him who is loved."[1]

Freedom, in both the Buddhist and the Christian sense, points to a new kind of morality which the law or empirical norms cannot measure. In both traditions the morality of freedom, if we may call it that, is compassion. Thus, after his enlightenment the Buddha chose to devote his life to teaching others rather than selfishly keeping his knowledge to himself. And Christianity is rooted in the affirmation, "Whoever would save his life will lose it; and whoever loses his life for my sake and the gospel's will save it" (Mark 8:35). Freedom in both Buddhism and Christianity is fulfilled in selfless service. Freedom is true compassion because the individual has overcome ego-defensiveness. He has become a new being where the old self or ego has been crucified.

True freedom for the religious man cannot be calculated. If it could, then it would not be freedom in the highest sense. The question, How free are you? is, therefore, meaningless from the standpoint of the final goal of both Christianity and Buddhism. One is either free or not free. In the old existence it is possible to calculate degrees of freedom but not in the new. Who is the freed man? Who is the saint? We really cannot tell. The Buddhist monastic discipline sees spiritual bragging as one of the worst offenses of the monk, and in the Christian tradition, humility is one of the cardinal virtues. Indeed, Kierkegaard said that you cannot tell the knight of faith from "the butcher, the baker, the candlestick maker." Religious freedom is an inner, spiritual quality, immeasurable but perhaps perceptible by those who have the "eyes to see and the ears to hear." There is a difference between freedom in the secular and religious senses. One of the contributions both the Buddhist and the Christian can make to the contemporary demand for political, social, and economic forms of freedom is to articulate these differences. Important as these forms of freedom are, they do not guarantee the freedom of the nirvanic or the resurrection life.

## *MOKṢA* (LIBERATION) AND *MARGA* (PATH)

In Chapter 3 we spoke of the movement of the religious life in both Christianity and Buddhism from an Old Creation to a New Creation, or from one mode of existence to a radically different one. Each mode of life is characterized in particular ways in the two traditions. In Theravāda Buddhism the basic symbolism is one of freedom versus bondage. The new life is one of freedom *(mokṣa)* from bondage and attachment to the objects of the sensate world. It is a freedom brought about above all by knowledge and equanimity; a state of being in which a person has overcome the powers of unconscious habits governing his life; a condition where the ordinary tensions threatening the moral life have been transcended; a mode of existence the Buddhist characterizes in terms of paranormal powers and extraordinary knowledge.

This ultimate freedom is designated by the term *nirvāna,* the final aim of the Buddhist life. It is not earned or achieved and in this sense subject to the will or intelligence of the Buddhist devotee. Rather it is realized as a consequence of following a path *(marga)* outlined by the Buddha himself. This path has three distinct elements: moral virtue *(sīla),* mental training *(samādhi),* and transcendental wisdom *(paññā).* We have already seen (Chapter 4) how within the Theravāda tradition the path moves progressively from good works to higher forms of mental cultivation and knowledge. The nature of both the goal and its path is indicated in the following dialogue in the *Saṁyutta-Nikāya* between the venerable Sariputta and a wandering truth seeker:

"Reverend Sariputta, . . . what, your reverence, is *nirvāna?"*

"Whatever, your reverence, is the extinction of passion, of aversion, of confusion, this is called *nirvāna.*"

"Is there a way, your reverence, is there a course for the realization of this *nirvāna?"*

"There is, your reverence."

"What is it, your reverence?"

"This Ariyan eightfold way itself is for the realization of *nirvāna;* that is to say, right views, right thought, right speech, right action, right mode of livelihood, right endeavor, right mindfulness, right concentration."[2]

The heart of the Buddhist path to freedom is mental training or meditation. The term "meditation" once evoked esoteric thoughts of monks in remote monasteries or incense-laden, darkened rooms. Today, however, we often hear of people practicing one form of meditation or another, transcendental meditation being one of the most popular forms. Some public school systems in this country have even adopted a brief period of meditation as part of the daily routine; meditation techniques are being used more and more by psychologists and psychiatrists as part of their psychotherapy: And in Christian circles an increase in the interest in spirituality has stimulated an increase in spiritual exercises and meditation. Fortunately, the mystique surrounding meditation is gradually wearing off, putting us in a better position to evaluate its possible roles within the Christian tradition.

What is the nature of Buddhist meditation? Is it the same as transcendental meditation, yoga, or other forms of mind training we associate with Asian religious tradition? We can, of course, find some similarities among many of these forms of discipline in their effects. For example, almost all of them describe meditation as producing a sense of calmness, and recently numerous kinds of scientific tests have shown that various forms of meditation have similar physiological effects, such as lowering breathing and metabolic rates, and changing brain-wave patterns.[3] Meditation practices within Buddhism produce similar effects, but we shall focus rather on the principles of Insight Meditation *(vipassanā)* which are basic to a variety of forms of mind training, both Buddhist and non-Buddhist.

The basic principle of Insight Meditation is awareness or mindfulness. While most of us think of meditation as a circumscribed course of mind training, in Buddhism the aim is to develop a total self-awareness, of which a more or less formal meditation program is only a part. In the broadest sense then, Insight Meditation is nothing more or less than constant attentiveness, overcoming our basic misunderstanding about ourselves and the world, cutting through illusion, and dispelling the mirage in order to see things as they really are rather than as what we mistakenly assume them to be. Buddhism assumes that most people look at the world and see what they want to see rather than what is really there. To quit kidding ourselves, to break the habit of looking and not seeing, of hearing but not listening, requires a special effort. Reflect on the number of times this past day, week, or month you have acted on the basis of inadequate or inaccurate information. Or, even more to the point, think about how many actions, gestures, and thoughts within the past hour or two were largely unconsciously and thoughtlessly motivated. Even such modest self-reflection helps to underscore the Buddhist insistence that our usual state is one of mindlessness, or lack of awareness. How can we break such patterns? How can we arrive at a state of total awareness, or mindfulness? How can the habits of perception and understanding be transformed? In the Buddhist view such an achievement does not come easily. We cannot go about our usual business in the same old way. Our ordinary routines too often only reinforce our uninformed and habituated patterns of perception, thought, and action. Like the athlete who works hard to get his body in shape in order to compete in a track meet, the Buddha teaches the necessity of training the mind in order to overcome our habitual ways of distorting reality.

One of the best-known Buddhist meditation programs in Theravāda Buddhism is based on a short text called the *Foundation of Mindfulness (Satipatthāna Sutta)*. It offers a systematic program for the development of mindfulness, or awareness, based on the principle of selective awareness. Selective awareness attempts to restrain the sensory inputs to the mind. Instead of the usual situation where we are bombarded by various tactile, audio, and visual stimuli, we shut out as many extraneous sensations, perceptions, and thoughts as possible in order to be aware of one thing at a time. Insight Meditation begins by putting the meditator by himself in a condition of relative sensory deprivation. He finds a quiet place and sits in a firm position (traditionally the lotus posture with one leg crossed over the other and both feet resting on the thighs) with the eyes partially or completely closed. Having so secluded himself, the meditator then focuses his attention on one object. As is true for most Indian types of mental training, Insight Meditation usually begins by focusing on the breathing process. The purpose of trying to be aware of only inhalation and exhalation is to become as fully conscious as possible of something which for most of us is usually a totally unconscious process. Only if we are having difficulty breathing because of a cold, or feel short of breath after a hard race, are we particularly aware of our breathing. Ordinarily, this process operates on a reflexive level.

Insight Meditation, then, functions to make us fully aware by beginning with breathing as the first meditation object. Once we are able to sit in quiet meditation totally aware of our inhalation and exhalation, of our breath entering and leaving our body, of periods of short and long breathing, we may then move on to other meditation objects. The *Satipatthāna Sutta* stipulates four different kinds of meditation objects: those of the body such as breathing; those having to do with sensations such as feelings of hot or cold, pleasure and pain; aspects of the consciousness such as hatred, lust, or ignorance, which give the mind a particular kind of bias or inclination; and, finally, ideas, especially those which form the core teachings of Buddhism, e.g., impermanence, notself. Thus, by moving from awareness of the body to sensations, to perceptions, and finally to ideas, the meditator takes a journey aimed at releasing him from blind attachments and ignorant assumptions.

Insight Meditation is a disciplined confrontation with the life processes as they actually occur. It does not depend upon intoxicants, hallucinogenic drugs, or other mind-altering chemicals. Rather, it cuts through the "vain imaginings" distorting and dominating our mind, by means of the vehicle of an objective understanding of things as they are, reached through a process of careful discrimination carried out in a controlled environment. For the dedicated practitioner the rewards are great. Yet one does not meditate to *gain* anything. One meditates simply to be able to *see* things as they really are in order to *be* as one really is. Self-understanding and self-acceptance are the results.

Within the Buddhist tradition many forms of mind training developed. One of the Zen sects of China and Japan made use of seemingly eccentric or paradoxical methods. For example, in the *koan* method the meditator was given a seemingly unanswerable question such as, What is the sound of one hand clapping? The practitioner pondered this problem and was called on to discuss his solution with the teacher. The Zen master's responses to the serious efforts of his disciple might take the form of totally ignoring him, hitting his student with a stick, or shoving him off the temple porch into a mud puddle. These unusual methods of provoking a solution to a rationally unsolvable problem force the meditator to persist in the face of an incomprehensible adversity. The point is that realization of spiritual truth is unlike the solution to an intellectual problem. Such truth is not a logical proposition to be solved and then dismissed. Rather, the realization of spiritual truth demands a radical change of thinking and of being.

Another method of meditation within the Buddhist tradition uses a *mantram,* a word or phrase repeated to focus attention. Perhaps the two best-known Buddhist *mantrams* are *Namu Amida Butsu,* "Homage to the Amida Buddha" (the Buddha thought by Japanese Buddhists of the Jodo Shin School to preside over the Pure Land or Western Paradise), and *Nam Myoho Renge Kyo,* "Homage to the Lotus Sutra," a *mantram* celebrating one of the most important scriptures in East Asian Buddhism. These phrases may be repeated audibly over and over again, or they may be mentally repeated as rosary-like beads are counted. Similar kinds of practice can be seen in Christianity, such as the repetition of the Hail Mary or the Jesus prayer in the Greek Orthodox monastic tradition. The verbal repetition of a phrase can have a hypnotic effect but that is not the goal. The use of the *mantram* in Buddhist meditation aims beyond trance to the understanding associated with Insight Meditation. In Buddhist meditation self-hypnosis is never an end in itself, although it may be a by-product of serious, intensive meditation. Buddhist texts also recognize that such trance states are potentially dangerous and for this reason intensive meditation is to be done only under the guidance of an accomplished meditation teacher.

The path of Buddhist meditation including both the *vipassanā,* or insight method, as well as the *samādhi,* or trance state method, can be characterized as nothing less than the creation of a new level of consciousness appropriate to a new level of nirvanic existence. It begins with awareness, leads to understanding, and in understanding things in their true nature one is freed from the ordinary limitations of sensate existence. One attains a state of unbornness, not-becomeness, not-madeness, uncompoundedness. In short, one reaches the condition of ultimate freedom—Nirvāna. Freedom, then, is both freedom *from* bondage to illusion and freedom *to* a completely other mode of existence. In a similar way Christian freedom is both the overcoming of bondage to sin and death and the attainment of a life likened to immortality.

## CHRISTIAN FREEDOM
## AND THE BUDDHIST PATH TO LIBERATION

While freedom accompanies the true saint in both the Buddhist and Christian views, differences in the symbolic frameworks can be profitably juxtaposed. In Buddhism, freedom is personified in the Buddha and in Christianity in the Christ. In Theravāda Buddhist countries the symbol most often used to depict the Buddha is a Buddha image where the hand position *(mudrā)* is that of subduing Mara, the tempter, who symbolizes the power of the sensate world. In Christianity the cross or crucifix is the most universal symbol of the Christ. As an overgeneralization to make a point, we might say that in Theravāda Buddhism the primary symbol denotes freedom born of non-attachment, whereas the crucifix denotes freedom born of involvement.

Non-attachment and involvement are not the exclusive hallmarks of Buddhism and Christianity respectively; rather, they form a polarity common to both traditions. The question is one of emphasis or focus. Buddhism emphasizes the one and Christianity the other. Indeed, in Protestant Christianity the theme of non-attachment is nearly lost. Whether in terms of Christology or Christian life and nurture, the theme of the Western Christian tradition has become largely one of involvement. Non-attachment, that quality so much a part of the concept of freedom in Buddhism, needs to be recaptured. We might illustrate this point first in terms of Christology.

While the early Christian councils sought to settle the theological question of the divine and human natures of Jesus the Christ, the quality of immanence and the humanity of Jesus rather than transcendence and his divinity have dominated modern American popular piety. For example, of the two principal Christian celebrations, Christmas and Easter, the former has captured the popular imagination. To be sure, there are sociological reasons for the dominance of Christmas over Easter, but for most Christians the Bethlehem manger evokes a warmer response than the Easter passion. Even at Easter, however, the human elements are easier to identify with than the divine ones. The agony of the cross, surprisingly enough, is really more comprehensible than the empty tomb. Besides, the latter is somewhat of an anticlimax lacking the drama of the former.

The liberal theology of the early twentieth century has long been displaced by more recent theological currents, but the popularity of Jesus, the moral example, epitomized by the American novel, *In His Steps,* is still close to the average American churchgoer's heart. It is part of the need to humanize the Christ figure, to involve him in our personal history as man-writ-large rather than as divine self-emptying (Phil. 2:8). Yet, as we have seen, the Christ as God becoming *suññatā* or God emptying himself is the most adequate Christological model for an understanding of the new being emerging from a theology of Christian-Buddhism dialogue. The Prologue to John's Gospel (John 1:1–5) and the Christological hymn in Phil. 2:5–11 complement each other in supporting the view of the Christ as the enactment of the New Creation.

In John's Prologue, Jesus is the *logos,* the creative Word ("all things were made through him") which was with God from the beginning of time ("In the beginning was the Word, and the Word was with God, and the Word was God"). God's Word becomes flesh not to limit itself, but to show the way to a new possibility of existence; it shows that the limitations of the flesh can be transcended, that mortality can put on immortality. This transformation takes place, in the words of Phil., ch. 2, when divinity becomes humanity in order that humanity may become divinity ("Have this mind in you which was in Christ Jesus, who, being in the form of God, ... took upon himself ... the likeness of men," Phil. 2:5, 6a, 7b). The Word made flesh and God come in the likeness of men are indeed symbolic of involvement, however, for the purpose of non-attachment. God's immanence, in other words, is man's transcendence. To glory in the Easter passion, to be touched by the baby Jesus, or to be inspired by the moral example of the righteous Christ, may be to miss the fundamental message of the incarnation. That message is one of self-emptying, of dying to be reborn, of not being attached to a life limited by the flesh and bound by the power of sin, of winning the freedom of true servanthood beyond the legal definition of righteousness, of being filled with a new life-power—the power *(dynamis)* of the Holy Spirit. Now let us turn to the practical question of the fashioning of our religious life in the light of such an ideal.

Contemporary Protestant church life often tends to be activity-oriented, so much so that its success may often be measured more in terms of committees and special interest groups than of the less visible and quantifiable quality of its spiritual life. The typical weekly calendar of events of mainline Protestant churches will probably include Scouts, men's and women's groups, Christian education and outreach committee meetings, but not Bible study or prayer groups. Furthermore, the average Protestant worship service represents a pell-mell rush for fifty to sixty minutes through hymns, prayers, and a more or less didactic sermon with little or no time for quiet, reflective meditation. As Lesslie Newbigin so cogently remarked over twenty years ago, the dynamic and creative Word of God tends to become a "question of doctrinal correctness."[4]

The church in America in our own day more or less reflects the time-rushed, secularized atmosphere of modern American culture. Yet, we cannot help sensing that the religious life of many Christians has become so pedestrian and humdrum that deep-felt needs for a more spiritually focused and disciplined life are not being met. This feeling was reinforced for me during the summer of 1975 when I helped lead an intensive week-long seminar on Christianity and Asian religions which included meditation practice. At the end of the week nearly everyone agreed that the meditation experience had greatly enhanced both the personal and group significance of the seminar, and that such a discipline could greatly enrich the spiritual life of the church.

Throughout its long history the Christian church has, of course, taken both personal and corporate religious disciplines quite seriously. The Gospels tell us that Jesus withdrew from his disciples to pray in the Garden of Gethsemane (Mark 14:32f.). Paul admonished the church to be vigilant as a corporate body and appealed to the brethren, "to present your bodies as a living sacrifice, holy and acceptable to God" (Rom. 12:1). Within the church as an institution, monastic and religious orders have most notably developed and preserved both individual and community religious disciplines. St. Anthony, generally regarded as the father of Christian monasticism, dedicated himself to a life of prayer and manual labor in the Egyptian desert after hearing a priest read the words of Jesus, "If you would be perfect, go, sell what you possess and give to the poor . . . ; and come, follow me" (Matt. 19:21). He was followed by others who sought to live a holy, set-apart life. In the opinion of Thomas Merton these early monks were not rejecting the world but were "men who did not believe in letting themselves be passively guided and ruled by a decadent state, and who believed that there was a way of getting along without slavish dependence on accepted, conventional values."[5]

St. Benedict's Rule (sixth century) formed the basis of monasticism in Western Christendom. It reflected the principal activities of study or reading, meditation and manual labor. Reading and meditation were related activities.

Reading was often aloud and texts were frequently composed or copied by dictation. Meditation was usually contemplation on Scripture and involved speaking, thinking, and remembering, i.e., the pronunciation of sacred words in order to retain them.[6] The attention given to meditation in the form of repetition of the psalms is demonstrated by the emphasis it receives in the opening chapters of Benedict's Rule. Other now classical spiritual exercises also developed out of the religious orders, the foremost being the *Spiritual Exercises* of St. Ignatius Loyola and the *Imitation of Christ* by Thomas à Kempis. Both are examples of what Evelyn Underhill characterizes as "practical mysticism," structured suggestions aimed at firsthand communion with God but also designed to meet the needs of the common man.

Despite the presence of rich contemplative traditions within the Christian church, their impact has been felt primarily in the religious orders that gave them birth. Furthermore, in the modern period contemplative orders have occupied an even more peripheral place in Catholic church life, and are nearly non-existent in Protestant circles. Yet, evidence from several quarters both inside and outside the church suggests that within the past five years there has been a renewal of interest in meditation, contemplation, and spiritual exercises. Certainly in the past decade a sizable number of non-Christian groups either closely or loosely tied to Asian spiritual and contemplative traditions have arisen and developed in this country. In both small and large towns and cities Transcendental Meditation, Krishna Consciousness or Sufi centers are likely to be found, and in more remote locations Zen and Tibetan Buddhist meditation groups are thriving. Within the church we find an upsurge of interest in devotional spirituality and contemplation ranging from increasing religious publications in this area to meditation instruction in local churches. Some of this interest within the church owes a clear debt to Buddhism. Thomas Merton, the Trappist monk at Gethsemani Abbey in Kentucky, was becoming more and more interested in Asian forms of spirituality before his untimely death in 1968, and William Johnston and Enomiya Lassalle, Jesuits serving in Japan, have been profoundly influenced by Zen Buddhism. Father Lassalle has been a practitioner of Zen meditation for several

decades and incorporates *zazen* into the Masses he cele-
brates at his simple, Zen-style church outside of Tokyo.[7] William Johnston's recent books, *Christian Zen* and *Silent
Music,* suggest ways Christian spirituality can derive benefit
from Buddhist meditation.

Among those involved in interreligious dialogue in this
country, Thomas Merton has probably contributed the most
to a Christian appreciation of Asian contemplative traditions.
He saw that contemplatives from various traditions could
communicate more openly on the basis of their experience
than theologians and philosophers on the level of abstract
ideas: "A little experience of such dialogue shows at once that
this [contact among contemplatives] is precisely the most
fruitful and the most rewarding level of ecumenical exchange. While on the level of philosophical and doctrinal
formulations there may be tremendous obstacles to meet, it
is often possible to come to a very frank, simple, and totally
satisfying understanding in comparing notes on the contemplative life, its disciplines, its vagaries, and its rewards. Indeed, it is illuminating to the point of astonishment to talk to
a Zen Buddhist from Japan and to find that you have much
more in common with him than with those of your own
compatriots who are little concerned with religion, or interested only in its external practice."[8] I wholeheartedly agree
with Merton, for my own experience with devout Buddhist
monks corroborates his claim.

Why can contemplatives come to such empathetic, mutual understanding? For Merton the answer lies in the fact
that contemplatives seek a direct intuition of reality, a "pure
awareness which is and must be the ground not only of all
genuine metaphysical speculation, but also of mature, sapi-
ential religious experience."[9] Contemplatives, therefore,
have a special contribution to make to interreligious dialogue
because they have a deeper insight into the inner and
spiritual ground which underlies all articulated differences
among religious traditions.[10] If Merton's position has merit,

then an appreciation of the Buddhist contemplative tradition should serve to provide us with both an unusual understanding of Buddhism and also new dimensions of Christian spirituality. What, then, are some of the ways in which the meditative traditions of Buddhism can contribute to our own religious life as well as to interreligious dialogue?

You will recall from our discussion of Insight Meditation that it proposed to open our eyes to the way things really are. What better starting point can one find for the religious life? As Christians we affirm that God accepts us *as we are;* yet, all too often we try to hide from ourselves. Self-deception may stem from our perceived inability to measure up to the self-image we have projected or that has been made for us by parents, teachers, and peers. Both psychological and spiritual health depends on our ability to cope with such images, to understand who we really are. Too often, our affirmation of God's forgiveness is not accompanied by self-understanding, with the consequence that our sense of inadequacy and guilt even intensifies. Merely to assert God's forgiveness as a theological axiom of the Christian faith does nothing for our spiritual well-being. Insight Meditation, with its emphasis on a systematic contemplation of our body, feelings, predispositions, and ideas can provide the framework in which the central affirmation of the Christian faith takes on concrete significance. Or, to put this proposition in terms more compatible with Buddhist teachings, mental training or spiritual exercises of the nature of Insight Meditation can help break the hold that erroneous and unfortunate self-images impose on us. To experience God's acceptance is to have plumbed the depths of my own being. Most of us come by such self-knowledge only as a result of a directed and concentrated effort. In our secularized culture this process most often happens in some non-religious context, i.e., group therapy, psychological analysis, rather than in the church. Too often conventional religious life contributes to this problem through both the nature of its activities and the superficiality with which its affirmations of faith are realized in the lives of its people. For these reasons many people outside the church judge its piety to be irrelevant.

I am not suggesting that churches be turned into meditation centers, or that the Christian's concern for social justice be transformed into myopic, navel-gazing sentimentality. Quite the contrary. I am in total agreement with Thomas Merton's continuous emphasis on the connection between the contemplative life and living in the world. In Buddhism and Christianity there is no inherent conflict between spirituality and action. Indeed, the two merge to perfection in compassion, the highest form of detached concern for others. The conflict between contemplation and action may exist logically or, perhaps, for those who have not engaged in contemplation. But, for those who have, meditation is as necessary a part of living in the world as physical exercise is for the athlete.

The role Insight Meditation can play in providing a framework for the realization of God's acceptance might be thought of in terms of grace. Conventionally we think of God's grace as something he *gives* and we *receive*. Yet, grace also has the meaning of gracefulness. To receive God's grace means to become grace-ful, to know ourselves not superficially but as God knows us in our innermost being, and in that knowledge to be completely one with our actions. To be graceful means to have overcome self-consciousness, to have negated the ego-defenses that made us awkward and out of place. In Merton's terms, to be graceful involves giving up attachments (to oneself) in order to be filled with the joy of God which then overflows to others.[11] To experience God's acceptance, to receive his grace may seem diametrically opposed to the practice of Insight Meditation. Yet, God's acceptance requires our own self-acceptance, and we cannot accept ourselves if we do not know who we are. Therefore, strange as it may seem, grace and self-knowledge have a necessary relationship to each other. To be grace-ful means to know oneself to the very depth of one's being. And, while the church cannot dispense grace, it can and should provide the context for the self-discovery necessary for its receipt. In short, the practice of Insight Meditation could be the occasion for the receipt of grace.

The first crucial role spiritual exercises could play as part of a Christian way to liberation could be to develop self-knowledge. A second could be to restore a new openness to the meaning of God's work in the world, or to dimensions of transcendence we had not seen, or had neglected. All of us have had the experience of looking at something familiar as though we were seeing it for the first time. It may have been something as ordinary as our home or an old friend, an occasion, we know not why, when we were startled out of a habitual way of perceiving. Our faith ought to be geared to such surprises, startling experiences, or revelations, but generally it is not. Too often we see things only on the surface or superficially rather than the way they really are.

The Rinzai Zen form of meditation using the *koan* meets this problem head on. The *koan* is a mental puzzle that cannot be resolved in an ordinary rational or logical manner, thereby forcing the student into a new perspective or point of view. *Koans* take many forms. Some are questions, others enigmatic stories, and still others seem relatively obvious in meaning.

> Two monks were arguing about a flag. One said: "The flag is moving."
> The other said: "The wind is moving."
> The sixth patriarch happened to be passing by. He told them: "Not the wind, not the flag; mind is moving."[12]

How does one solve this *koan?* Not by reason but by living with it and identifying with it until one forgets oneself in the discovery of new levels of meaning to life. Perhaps the closest analogue to the resolution of a *koan* is that sense of "Eureka!" when we have made a new discovery and are overcome by a sense of elation.

William Johnston suggests that our faith would be enriched if we looked at much of the Bible as a *koan*.[13] Certainly, one of the traditional modes of Christian meditation was contemplation of the Scriptures. Johnston, however, is suggesting a change in the traditional use of Scripture as an object of meditation. If we looked at particular Bible passages as *koans* to be pondered and lived with until a new understanding dawned in our consciousness, our faith would be more profound. During my own meditation experience in a Rinzai meditation center in Kyoto my teacher gave me as a *koan,* "Who is the I in the phrase, 'I am who I am'?" Bible scholars can answer this question rather easily from the perspective of historical criticism, but what does it mean for faith? That is, what would it mean if we pondered that phrase, meditated on it day and night until suddenly, one day, quite unexpectedly, the answer was there before our eyes—not a reasoned answer, but one that opened up a whole new dimension of living, one that wrought a transformation of the spirit? As Johnston observes: "Put aside for a while your critical faculties of reasoning and arguing. Stop asking whether Jesus did or did not walk on the waters, whether there was or was not a star to guide the Wise Men. Stop asking what it all means; because what it means is less important than what it does to you. Forget all the complications and let the words enter the visceral area of your body, where they will finely and delicately begin to act, to live, to change you."[14]

The New Testament has its own particular koanic form in the parables, and some of the stories of the saints—like the Hasadic and Sufi tales of Judaism and Islam—are koanic in nature. The nature of the parables, as Jesus indicated, is that they have a hidden meaning obvious only to those who know the truth (i.e., are in faith): "To you it has been given to know the secrets of the kingdom of God; but for others they are in parables, so that seeing they may not see, and hearing they may not understand" (Luke 8:10). To be able to understand the parables means that one must comprehend the meaning of the focal *koan* of the New Testament—the incarnation. To ponder the incarnation as a *koan* rather than as a paradox made pedestrian by theologians may serve to enliven and deepen our faith. For example, a picture of the crucifixion painted from a koanic perspective might depict Jesus with a smile on his face. Do you find the suggestion offensive? Is that not the point of the crucifixion—to be an offense? You simply had not thought of the crucifixion as an offense in these terms. That is the value of dialogue!

Grace and faith are the two pillars of the Christian notion of liberation. We assume that we know the meaning of these two concepts. Indeed, we might even have spent considerable amounts of time studying about them. Yet, as I have suggested, contemplation and meditation as practiced in Buddhism open up new dimensions of life in the spirit and of understanding the dynamics of Christian liberation.

## Chapter 6

# A Kingdom of Priests and a Holy Nation

"And I will take you for my people, and I will be your God; and you shall know that I am the LORD your God, who has brought you out from under the burdens of the Egyptians." (Ex. 6:7.)

From a sociological point of view religion serves as the social cement of a given society or social group, helping it to meet life's crises, providing an account of its origins, and offering ethical norms sanctioning acceptable behavior. Of all the world's great religions Judaism stands out for the focal significance of community, both as a historical reality and as a theological concept. In the dual events of the exodus of the Hebrew peoples from captivity in Egypt and the Mosaic covenant between the Children of Israel and the God, Yahweh, on Mt. Sinai, Yahweh emerges as the God who establishes a special community of chosen people who owe their existence to him.

## CHOSEN PEOPLE

"In the third new moon, after the children of Israel had gone forth out of the land of Egypt, on that day they came into the wilderness of Sinai . . . and pitched their tents in the wilderness; and there Israel camped before the mountain. And Moses went up to God, and the LORD called to him out of the mountain, saying, 'Thus you shall say to the house of

Jacob, and tell the people of Israel: You have seen what I did to the Egyptians, and how I bore you on eagles' wings and brought you to myself. Now therefore, if you will obey my voice, and keep my covenant, you shall be my possession among all peoples; for all the earth is mine, and you shall be to me a kingdom of priests, and a holy nation.' " (Ex. 19:1–6.)

The Mosaic covenant is an agreement between the Hebrew peoples and the God, Yahweh. In exchange for Yahweh's leading the Hebrews out of Egyptian bondage, preserving them through the trails of a wilderness wandering, and helping them settle in Canaan, they pledged to worship no other gods. They also pledged not to make any graven image of him, to keep the seventh day as the sabbath, and to obey such laws as not taking human life, not committing adultery, not stealing, not bearing false witness, and not coveting. (Ex. 20:1–17.)

This covenant, which formed the fundamental bond among several Hebrew tribes, was renewed at an annual ceremony at the town of Shechem (cf. Josh., ch. 24). The nation, or the federated community of Hebrew clans, was therefore brought into being and continued to exist through their loyalty to Yahweh.

The exodus/Sinai experiences symbolize a dramatic enactment of the creation theme, of bringing into being a nation that previously had suffered because it was disunited. Scattered in Canaan where they had settled, some taken into servitude in Egypt, the Hebrew tribes had little sense of common purpose until they were bound together in common loyalty to Yahweh. They depicted this event as an emergence from darkness and bondage into freedom and light. The flight through the Red Sea and the episode of the wilderness wandering point to a preliminary period of purification and testing prior to the ratification of the covenant on Mt. Sinai and the establishment of a code for a new way of life. The mountain itself is symbolic of the power of God which had brought the new nation into being and thereby opened up new possibilities previously unknown. On it the covenant was made and the law promulgated creating a community dedicated to Yahweh.

The nation Israel, or the federated community of Hebrew clans, was born as a community distinct from its Canaanite surroundings. Throughout its history there has existed a tension between the particular and the universal, the exclusive and the inclusive nature of the community. Within the prophetic tradition this polarity is manifest. Universalism is declared in First Isaiah: "It shall come to pass in the latter days that the mountain of the house of the LORD shall be established as the highest of the mountains, and shall be raised above the hills; and all the nations shall flow to it, and many peoples shall come, and say: 'Come, let us go up to the mountain of the LORD, to the house of the God of Jacob; that he may teach us his ways and that we may walk in his paths'" (Isa. 2:2–3a). The particularistic focus occurs in Hosea: "I will make for you a covenant on that day. . . . And I will betroth you to me for ever; I will betroth you to me in righteousness and in justice, in steadfast love, and in mercy. I will betroth you to me in faithfulness; and you shall know the LORD" (Hos. 2:18–20). Institutionally a similar tension is reflected in the different outlooks of Reformed versus Orthodox Judaism, and the ardent Zionist versus the non-Zionist.

## THE BODY OF CHRIST

The more particularistic side of the Hebrew sense of community was transformed by the collapse of the kingdoms of Israel and Judah in the eighth and sixth centuries B.C. and the creation of a Jewish diaspora in Babylonia and elsewhere in the ancient Middle East. Some of the later Old Testament prophets such as Second Isaiah, Jeremiah, and Ezekiel began to depict the covenant relationship in more universal terms (Jer. 31:31ff.). They foresaw a messiah or redeemer not only for the Jews but for all nations (Isa. 56:3ff.). Deutero-Isaiah's vision of the Suffering Servant in particular influenced the early Christian community's conception of Jesus Christ: "He was despised and rejected by men; a man of sorrows, and acquainted with grief; and as one from whom men hide their faces he was despised, and we esteemed him not. Surely he has borne our griefs and carried our sorrows; yet we esteemed him stricken, smitten by God, and afflicted" (Isa. 53:3–4).

The New Testament writers saw Jesus not only as a savior of the Jews but of all nations. For example, in the Christological hymn in Philippians, we read: "And being found in human form he humbled himself and became obedient unto death, even death on a cross. Therefore God has highly exalted him and bestowed on him the name which is above every name, that at the name of Jesus every knee should bow, in heaven and on earth and under the earth" (Phil. 2:8–10). Indeed, while Jesus himself was a Jew, in the New Testament he is portrayed as a critic of Jewish temple practices and as one who appealed to the universal virtues of compassion, humility, and service above the Jewish law. The law, thus, becomes subsumed under the great commandment, "Love one another as I have loved you" (John 15:12).

In the covenant terminology of the Old Testament, Jesus represents a new covenant based on a new order of creation of which Jesus is the initiator. We have already seen (Chapter 3) how Jesus represents a new being or new humanity. In the context of community and covenant Jesus is represented by the church, the body of believers who have become Christ's people, i.e., the new humanity. The church in this sense is the body of Christ. Although the church is composed of individuals with different backgrounds and talents, they are united in a common loyalty, a common participation in a new life in Christ signaled by baptism into his death and resurrection, and a common obligation of service.

Instead of the metaphor of the chosen people united by legal covenant, the metaphor of the body of Christ comes to stand for the community of those who in their faith or act of self-emptying have come to realize their ultimate oneness. The apostle Paul gives expression to this metaphor in his letters to the church at Rome and Corinth: "For just as the body is one and has many members, and all the members of the body, though many, are one body, so it is with Christ. For by one Spirit we were all baptized into one body—Jews or Greeks, slaves or free—and all were made to drink of one Spirit" (I Cor. 12:12–13); "For as in one body we have many members, and all the members do not have the same function, so we, though many, are one body in Christ, and individually members one of another" (Rom. 12:4–5).

In his letters to the Romans and Corinthians, Paul insists on the substantive unity of the church as the body of Christ. There is, however, a functional diversity rooted in the fact that the historic church is composed of different individuals. Churches as historic entities or sociological institutions vary greatly. However, organically they are one body of Christ, a new humanity which has seen the power of God reflected in the Christ event.

The Christian community is heir to both the Old Covenant tradition of the chosen people as well as the New Covenant tradition of the new humanity, and the tension between the particular/exclusive and universal/inclusive is rooted in this polarity. Paul can say to the Romans that God shows no partiality whether one is a Jew or a Greek (Rom. 2:10–11) and to the Corinthians that neither circumcision nor uncircumcision counts for anything (I Cor. 7:19). Yet, although God alone is the judge of the righteous and those who have been baptized into Christ are all sons of God, Paul also writes that immoral and wicked people cannot be tolerated and are to be driven from the church (I Cor. 5:9–13).

The history of Christianity as well as the history of Judaism can be viewed from various facets, both doctrinal and institutional, of the particular/universal theme. Furthermore, this theme is closely related to the polarity of immanence and transcendence. These themes are not identical, but often we find a linkage between particularity and transcendence, and universality and immanence. As theologians (e.g., Paul Tillich) and sociologists (e.g., Robert Bellah) have pointed out, religion necessarily moves between such poles. The tension between church and monastery in the medieval period or the recent debate over the Hartford Appeal and the Boston Affirmations[1] reflects this dialectic. Buddhism shares a similar tension between the poles of the particular and universal in regard to its conception of community. We shall examine these two poles and then move on to see how the Buddhist notion of community might help us recast our own.

## THE ASSEMBLY (*SANGHA*)
## OF THE FOUR QUARTERS

Within the Theravāda Buddhist tradition there is a rough parallel to the particularistic and universalistic Biblical themes in regard to the conception of community. The particularistic theme emerges as the *bhikkhu sangha,* the brotherhood of monks; the universalistic theme is found in the *catursangha,* the *sangha* of the four quarters, which includes both monks and laity. While the former is the best known, the latter deserves more attention than it has received, especially in relationship to the historic and contemporary role of the Buddhist *sangha.*

The Pāli term *sangha* literally means an assembly, group, or community that has been brought together (*saṅ + hṛ*). In its early Buddhist usage it denoted a group that had come together to study the teachings *(dhamma)* of the Lord Gotama, the Buddha. And, within the historical context of early Buddhism it probably denoted a group governed by a republican rather than a monarchical form of government. Perusal of the early Theravāda scriptures shows that the distinction between *bhikkhu,* one who had renounced the lay life to become a disciple of the Buddha, and *gihin,* one who continued in the status of lay life, was relatively informal in regard to Buddha *dhamma*. That is, we find some stories of laymen who are pious devotees of the Buddha with a profound understanding of his teachings (e.g., Anathapindika), and also stories of laymen who became *arahants* and attained Nirvāna. Consistent with this tradition is chapter 25 of the *Dhammapāda* which defines a monk *(bhikkhu)* not as one who has simply become a member of the order but one who is restrained in body and mind, humble, pure, not slothful, delights in the *dhamma*, behaves with loving-kindness, and "illumines this world like the moon freed from a cloud."

In other words, to gain a profound understanding of the Buddha's teachings and even to attain the highest goal of complete equanimity (Nirvāna), it was not necessary to become a *bhikkhu*. The distinction between *bhikkhu* and *gihin* was, therefore, a relative one denoting those who had given up the householder way to live in a community with the Buddha and those who still lived as householders. This distinction was older than Buddhism and was simply adapted by the early Buddhist community from its cultural environment.

The early Buddhist *sangha*, therefore, was composed of two groups, monk and layman. Both were disciples of the Buddha, sought to understand the truth of his teachings, and to practice his distinctive way to the realization of peace and freedom *(mokṣa)*. This was the *sangha* of the four quarters, which was universal in nature, as the title itself implies. It did not make a qualitative distinction between an elite group of religious virtuosi, and laymen who were spiritually second-class citizens. It was a community brought together by a common *dhamma*, or truth, which the founder, known as the Buddha, had realized and taught.

The Buddha-dhamma, from this perspective, is the functional equivalent of the body of Christ or the new humanity in the Christian tradition. It denotes not only the Buddhist scriptures or empirical teachings of the Buddha but the truth. Consequently, just as the Christian becomes a new being by his participation in the body of Christ, so the Buddhist becomes a new being by his participation in Buddha-dhamma. The *sangha* of the four quarters may therefore be depicted as the embodiment of Buddha-dhamma in the same way that the church is the embodiment of Christ.

This inclusive Buddhist community has had several important historical ramifications. Buddhism emerged as a national church in India under the emperor Asoka, who was perceived as a universal monarch or *cakkavattin* (literally, one who turns the wheel of the law). The *cakkavattin* ideal has been an important counterpart to the spread of Buddhism throughout Southeast Asia. Buddhism in Sri Lanka, Burma, Thailand, Cambodia, and Laos has functioned as an inclusivistic national religion, often coupled with the *cakkavattin* ideal. Furthermore, Buddhism in these countries has a remarkable doctrinal similarity based on a commonly held *dhamma*. The neo-Buddhist movement in India begun under the inspirational leadership of Dr. Ambedkar is trying to break down the exclusivistic tradition of the Hindu caste system and has had a remarkable success among the outcasts, or Harijans. While the movement may be interpreted largely on sociological grounds, it is not inconsistent with the universalistic aspect of the concept of community in Buddhism.

## THE ASSEMBLY (*SANGHA*)
## OF THE MENDICANTS

While the "community of the four quarters" or the universal brotherhood of those who call themselves Buddhists is not absent from the Theravāda Buddhist tradition, the *bhikkhu sangha* has dominated it. The community of monks or mendicants has been distinctive and particularistic in that they have been set apart from the way of life of the householder and have been idealized as a religious elite in the pursuit of Nirvāna.

*Bhikkhus*—so they call you *"bhikkhus."* Well, see to it that you make this become a true word and your profession become genuine; see to it that your religious life becomes not barren but of great fruit. Train yourselves to become this and then that. Nor rest content thinking that what is done is enough and that there is nothing further to be done. I declare to you, I protest to you: Let there be no falling back in your aim while there is something further to be done. And what is there further to be done? First, to become conscientious and scrupulous; thereafter, successively, to become pure in deed, speech, thought and mode of living; to become guarded as to the senses; to become moderate in eating; to become intent on diligence; to become mindful and circumspect; to become possessed of the six-fold super-knowledge. . . . When they are finally accomplished the *bhikkhu* can finally say: lived is the Brahma-faring, done what was to be done. *(Majjhima-Nikāya,* i. 271ff.)[2]

At its best the monastic community is the personification of both the Buddha ideal and the Nirvāna ideal. On the one hand, the *sangha* is the compassionate teacher embodying the teacher's *dhamma;* on the other, it is the community of those who practice the disciplines leading to the attainments of calmness and dispassion. While, in actual fact, the *sangha* may not live up to this ideal, it still continues to represent it. At the very least it offers a context for the pursuit of holiness for those who wish to seek it.

The activity of the Theravāda monkhood may be roughly divided into two kinds: those which promote the well-being of the *bhikkhu sangha* itself and those dedicated to the well-being of lay society. The first includes those disciplines aimed at individual self-perfection, e.g., study, meditation, as well as communal rules that preserve the integrity of the community such as observance of the monastic code (227 *vinaya* rules). Ideally the monastic order maintains a balance between the two, providing an environment for growth in individual spirituality coupled with sympathetic concern for those who must live in continuous, close proximity with one another for long periods of time. If the *bhikkhu sangha* lives up to such an ideal—and it would be unfair to say that it usually does—then it becomes a community that encourages the highest form of individualism (e.g., spiritual excellence), but does so as part of a corporate body where the individual submits his own will to the collective good.

The Buddhist monkhood as a distinctive community has never been cut off from the world. From the beginning its mendicant nature necessitated dependence on lay support. The Theravāda scriptures *(suttas)* are filled with stories of lay persons who seek out the advice of the Buddha, and who provide places for the monks to find shelter. Hence, although the community is a place where one can withdraw from worldly occupations to seek a higher wisdom, the monastic order and lay society had mutual obligations. In particular the order as an embodiment of virtue shared its merit primarily through teaching the *dhamma* in exchange for material support by the laity. Later this reciprocal exchange of spiritual blessing and material support became the focal meaning of many rituals. Traditionally, however, the virtue of the monastic order was its participation in *dhamma* which it shared through teaching. Hence, one of the principal services provided by the monastic order was one of education, a role the *bhikkhu sangha* monopolized until the colonial period. Even today in Thailand approximately one third of the school age children are in monastery schools. Indeed, if it were not for the monastery schools, many of Thailand's poor would be receiving little or no education at all.

The teaching function of the Buddhist monastic order is one of many practical roles it performs. Above all, the monastery is identified as a center for a wide variety of lay-centered religious celebrations, ceremonies, and festivals. In traditional Thailand the monastery also still functions as dispensary, retirement center, orphanage, bank, etc. In more innovative and controversial roles monks provide leadership in community development and urban environmental projects.

In short, the *bhikkhu sangha* revolves around a tripartite relationship between its stated higher goal (Nirvāna), its own distinctive community life, and its various relationships with lay society.

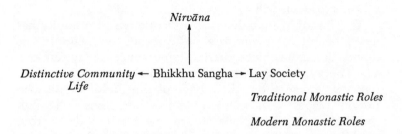

*Nirvāna*

*Distinctive Community* ← Bhikkhu Sangha → Lay Society
*Life*

*Traditional Monastic Roles*

*Modern Monastic Roles*

In contemporary Asia the Theravāda *sangha* faces immense challenges on several fronts. In Ceylon and Burma colonial rule significantly weakened the structure of the monastery order. The Indochina war has left Buddhist institutions in Laos, Cambodia, and Vietnam scarred and battered. Rapid social, economic, and political changes in Thailand are nearly more than monastic leadership can cope with. The ability of the monastic order to meet this new situation will depend on its ability to maintain itself as a distinctive locus of holiness, strengthen its own leadership and reform its internal structures, and continue to challenge the assumptions behind modernization and Westernization from the perspective of its ultimate goals rather than mere institutional self-preservation.

Yahweh called the Hebrew clans to be not only a nation but a "holy priesthood." This call was part of its role as a distinctive community among the Canaanites as well as throughout its entire history. The apostle Paul saw the church as a distinctive body, an organic whole likened to the body of Christ. In Buddhism, the *bhikkhu sangha* has been

that part of the community most dedicated to the perpetua-
tion of the distinctive religious traditions of Buddhism. Is
there in the Buddhist notion of the nature of a distinctive
religious community a lesson for the contemporary Christian
church?

## CHRISTIAN *SANGHA*

In a prophetic statement published in 1966, Julio Sabanes,
professor at the Union Theological Seminary in Buenos Aires,
observed that at that moment in Christian history the church
stood at a crossroads. A particular doctrine offers a key to a
new understanding of the Christian faith; the doctrine of
community is the particular key for our own day.[3] Sabanes'
observation was prophetic in the sense that a decade later
the loss of Christian community and the consequent need to
plumb the meaning of that concept seems considerably more
urgent and demanding. The early 1960's seemed promising.
We had not yet known the assassinations of President
Kennedy and Martin Luther King; few Americans were even
aware of Vietnam; we had successfully challenged the Sovi-
ets over missile installations in Cuba; and the economy of the
New Frontier was booming. The following decade brought
domestic violence, the sordid memory of Vietnam, and the
corruption of Watergate. By the time America celebrated its
Bicentennial it was much less certain about itself, and many
American churches shared a similar uncertainty. The need to
capture a new sense of the meaning of Christian community
has seemingly never been more timely.

Surprisingly, perhaps, the New Testament term *koinos*
and its derivatives bear some fundamental resemblances to
the Buddhist term *sangha*—viz., *koinōnos,* partner or companion; *koinōneō,* to be a friend or companion, or to share
with others; *koinōnia,* a group of people sharing in a new
reality or in the Christian sense the reality established by
God in Christ. Those who share in Christian community, who

are partners in this fellowship, share in both the suffering and the promise of Christ: "that I may know him and the power of his resurrection, and may share *(koinōnian)* his sufferings" (Phil. 3:10). To live with Christ (Rom. 6:8) is to suffer with him (Rom. 8:17) and to be crucified with him (Gal. 2:19) in order to share in the blessings of the gospel (I Cor. 9:23) and the divine nature of Christ (II Peter 1:4). What might the notion of a Christian *sangha* as we have examined it in Buddhism add to this already profoundly rich concept of *koinōnia?*

The concept of a Christian *sangha* is, first of all, a particularistic community of loyal followers of Jesus, those who have known the power of the New Creation in their own lives, and who seek by practice, study, and devotion to remain faithful to his teaching. Secondly, it is universalistic in that Jesus did not intend his message exclusively for one group, race, or nation, and furthermore, because the moral consequence of a life of faith is an unqualified compassion or *agapē*. As Paul wrote to the church at Corinth, love *(agapē)* is the aim of the Christian and the perfect expression of the Christian life. "Love bears all things, believes all things, hopes all things, endures all things." (I Cor. 13:7.) The two pillars of the Christian *sangha* would be, therefore, practice rooted in contemplation and service based on compassion. What the Buddhist notion of *sangha* adds is an emphasis on the commitment to a religious discipline aimed at understanding things as they really are, and a view of religion as a path or a way that includes appropriate degrees and levels of preparation culminating in a new mode of existence.

What kind of institution would a Christian *sangha* be? First, it may be helpful to suggest some possible models. One model that comes to mind would resemble some of the contemporary spiritual groups with which I have become acquainted. These groups have a strong sense of community solidarity based on a variety of shared experiences focused around spiritual exercises and meditation, a highly respected leader, and a more or less well-defined body of teachings.

Some of these communities have sought relatively remote locations, but most of them are in cities and towns. Some groups have a variety of centers. For example, Trungpa Rimpoche, a popular teacher of Tibetan Buddhism, has established a meditation community in Vermont, study centers in several cities, and a degree-granting educational program in Boulder, Colorado.

Another model with possible correlation to a Christian *sangha* would be the Buddhist monastic institution in a country like Thailand. Except in large, cosmopolitan cities, the Thai monastery continues as the center of the community. In addition to being the place where celibate monks live and practice religious disciplines, it is also a center of worship for the laity, a school, and a focal point for community activities. Perhaps the closest parallel to such a religious institution in the West would be pre-Reformation cathedral foundations in England under which Augustinian friars conducted schools and carried out other types of service efforts.

I do not mean to suggest a return to a medieval or premodern religious institutional model; but rather that the Christian *sangha* would be a center of spiritual culture functioning within the tripartite matrix of the New Creation in Christ, the distinctive community, and the world:

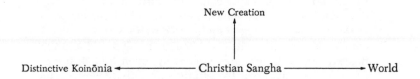

New Creation

Distinctive Koinōnia ◄─────── Christian Sangha ─────► World

Like the *bhikkhu sangha* in Thailand the Christian *sangha* would provide opportunities for study and reflection, contemplation and meditation, worship and devotion, and service growing out of understanding and compassion. Like the best of the spiritual communities in contemporary America, it would be a center of shared experience enhancing both the individual's growth and development as a spiritual being and the community's sense of its own uniqueness and its self-awareness as part of a wider brotherhood. A Christian *sangha* would also value simplicity ("Cast off useless burdens in order better to bear those of your fellow men unto Christ your Lord," *The Rule of Taizé*) and interior silence ("Interior silence requires first of all to forget one's self, to quiet discordant voices, and to master obsessing worry in the perpetual re-beginning of a man who is never discouraged because always forgiven," *The Rule of Taizé*).

What would the Christian *sangha* look like as an institution? I cannot answer that question, but whatever shape it would take its responsibility would be to fashion a way *(marga)* to a higher righteousness, a path to freedom, or, as Thomas Merton puts it, away from shadows to reality:

> They have not come to the monastery to escape from the realities of life but to find those realities: they have felt the terrible insufficiency of life in a civilization that is entirely dedicated to the pursuit of shadows.
>
> What is the use of living for things that you cannot hold on to, values that crumble in your hands as soon as you possess them, pleasures that turn sour before you have begun to taste them, and a peace that is constantly turning into war? Men have not become . . . [monks] merely out of a hope for peace in the next world: something has told them with unshakable conviction that the next world begins in this world and that heaven can be theirs now, very truly, even though imperfectly, if they give their lives to the one activity which is the beatitude of heaven.
>
> That activity is love: the clean, unselfish love that does not live on what it gets but on what it gives; a love that increases by pouring itself out for others, that grows by self-sacrifice and becomes mighty by throwing itself away.[4]

Our dialogue with Buddhism in this chapter and throughout the book has intended both to illumine what is fundamental to the Christian faith and to challenge the way we understand and practice that faith. We have suggested here that Buddhism's contribution to a renewed appreciation of Christian community lies in the particular conception of the *sangha* as the embodiment of the founder's teaching; its understanding of the community as the locus of spiritual disciplines aimed at understanding; and the tripartite matrix that intersects the Buddhist monastic order in both its universal and particular dimensions.

# Chapter 7

# A Buddhist View
# of Christianity

In the five preceding chapters we have attempted to reexamine Christianity in the light of a sympathetic study of selected facets of Buddhism. In this final chapter the dialogue between Christianity and Buddhism continues on another level. A contemporary Buddhist monk examines Christianity from his own unique point of view. The monk is Bhikkhu Buddhadāsa, Thailand's most creative monastic mind.[1]

The following selections from Buddhadāsa are taken from his Thompson lectures delivered at the Thailand Theological Seminary in 1971. As will be evident from these passages, Buddhadāsa has not made a thorough and systematic study of Christianity. Rather, he interprets Christianity from the particular vantage point of one whose sense of genuine religiousness or spirituality transcends the particular "isms" that have divided religious persons from one another. As we read these selections we should keep in mind that Buddhadāsa has not been educated in Western critical method, nor, for that matter, has he ever traveled outside an Asian country. Consequently, his insight into Christianity stems from his particular experience as a Thai Buddhist and his understanding of the nature and function of religion. We shall first let Buddhadāsa speak for himself. Then, in the concluding portion of this chapter, we shall enter into dialogue with this renowned monk.

## BUDDHADĀSA ON CHRISTIANITY

Let us look at Christianity from the Buddhist viewpoint. For brevity's sake, we will refer only to the Bible. We assume that the fundamentals of Christianity are found in this text and cannot be separated from it. First, the actual Biblical text must be considered. We Buddhists approach scripture like Christian scholars do; we too do not attribute equal authority or equal importance to all religious texts. In the Bible, the Old Testament contains creation accounts and the history of the Hebrew people, but it does not include any specifically Christian teaching. However, the New Testament presents the way taught by Jesus Christ which leads to man's highest state, his salvation. We will therefore limit our discussion to this part of the Bible.

In my personal opinion, the Christians of Jesus' time could well have followed his teaching without paying much attention to the Old Testament. Indeed Jesus himself probably urged his disciples not to concern themselves unduly with the Hebrew scriptures, but to concentrate on his practical guide to emancipation. The same can be said for those disciples of the Buddha who were alive during his lifetime; many realized the Noble Path and attained the Fruition without knowing the details of the Tripiṭaka [the canon of Theravāda Buddhism]. In fact, these texts were not compiled until after the Mahāparinibbāna (the passing away of the Buddha) of the Awakened One. The Tripiṭaka records many variations of practical teachings and methods aimed at the extinction of suffering, and extends to twenty times the length of the entire Bible. Although much shorter in length, the New Testament, too, provides enough guidance for a person's emancipation from suffering. . . .

The caution evidenced by Jesus in relying on the Old Testament is similar to the attitude of the Enlightened One. Emphasizing the value of practice, he discouraged his disciples from discussing impractical problems such as: Is a person reborn after death or not? What is it that is reborn? How is one reborn? The Compassionate One gave no answer to these futile speculations, and called questions about God and heaven "unanswerable." Instead he constantly stressed the value of the following inquiries: How do different kinds of suffering arise? What is it that causes suffering? [How may it be removed?] According to the Buddha, the answers to these questions are revealed directly through spiritual experience. In a person's own life he will see that his suffering results solely from his inability to reach the absolute truth, called Dhamma [*dharma* is the Sanskrit form of *dhamma*] or God. That truth is this: Whenever and wherever the feeling that one's *self belongs to oneself* arises, then and there suffering arises. But when there is no such feeling, when self belongs rather to Dhamma or to God, then there arises no suffering.

When a Brahmana (religious practitioner) attains the ability to destroy his feeling of selfishness, he is freed from suffering and is therefore content and satisfied; he has no need to inquire about rebirth or heaven. He has no concern for these questions because his happiness or selflessness is incomparably superior to the kind of happiness reputedly experienced in the various heavens. In this state of experience the Brahmana has no ego-self remaining to die, to be born again, or to suffer. Nature alone is left, by itself, without death or birth. Translated into conventional language, this state may be called the attainment of the Deathless (*amatadhamma*) or God. A person is said to have reached God or become one with God when his attachment to self is destroyed, and his heart and mind enlightened with the illuminating rays of God, the absolute truth (*paramdhamma*). He who is one with God has been given a new, different life. If a person achieves absolute selflessness, he is permanently free; there is nothing more for him to do. His religious practice is complete.

Without wasting time in the study of unnecessary things,

one should practice without delay to gain this highest truth. Study should be pursued only to solve problems of immediate concern. It should focus on one single point—how to eliminate the craving that gives rise to I-ness and my-ness and establish purity of mind. I am fully convinced that the founders of the world religions urged their followers, out of compassion, not to study unnecessary things. Even the few pages devoted to the Sermon on the Mount in the Gospel of Matthew embody all the practical means for attaining freedom from suffering. One could possibly ignore the rest of the New Testament, not to mention the Old Testament.

Many Christian leaders, however, preach their religion without mentioning the essential meaning of Christianity. Buddhist monks, too, often expound only the outward forms of Buddhism, without grasping the essence of Dhamma, the ridding of attachment to I and my. In one of the Pāli *suttas* the Buddha declares the core of Brahmacarya (the Holy Life) to be emancipation *(vimutti)* or salvation. Wisdom *(paññā)* is the wood surrounding the pith; meditation *(samādhi)* is the bark around the wood; morality *(sīla)* is the outermost dry bark; and gain, honor, fame, and even heaven are but the fallen leaves. Religious teaching these days does not touch the core of religion; that is why people of different faiths are so disparate and argumentative.

Both the Tripiṭaka and the Bible include sections which, while interesting, are not crucial and may be omitted. The only persons who might object to this procedure are scholars and teachers, and those who wish simply to be well-versed in the scriptures. Speaking to this point, the Buddha once said while holding a handful of leaves, "The things known to the Tathāgata are as numerous as the leaves in the forest, but the things I teach are equal only to this handful of leaves." Jesus spoke only a few words to the twelve disciples; even God's revelations to Moses and Abraham were brief. It appears, then, that the crucial response to the truth consists in faith and practice, not in lengthy discourse. In time, however, the compilation and revision of scriptures has resulted in a large canon, often tedious to study. Furthermore, prolonged learning of the Tripiṭaka or the Bible inhibits the progress of a person who wishes to realize the essence of religion. Many modern scholars have consequently lost sight of the important points in a jungle of scriptural facts. In order to revive the most necessary and practical religious truths, conferences of religious persons must periodically be convened to discuss religion in a new light and to promote an understanding among the general populace of the relevance of religion for a meaningful life in our modern world.

Let us now compare Christianity with Buddhism. How do these two religions differ? From the Buddhist viewpoint, it is important to know whether Christianity teaches self-help or whether it emphasizes a person's reliance on external help. What does it mean for a Christian to receive help given by another? If receiving another person's help means acting on his advice, would that be called self-help or external help? According to the common understanding of Christianity, the answer to these questions is simply that everything depends on the will of God. We cannot help ourselves without the help of God. Buddhism, however, maintains that we do help ourselves; we act by ourselves and consequently receive the results of our actions, distributed not by God but by the law of *karma.* There is no personal God who lives in heaven and controls the destiny of human beings. [People control their own lives.] In conventional language, then, Christianity is a religion that emphasizes external help while Buddhism stresses self-help. This apparent impasse leaves little possibility for dialogue.

But if we speak in Dhamma-language, from the viewpoint of the absolute truth, mutual understanding and comparison become feasible. On that level God and the law of *karma* are one and the same [in that both govern the results of men's actions]. If a person performs his duties properly, keeping the law of *karma* in mind, he will receive good results. Doing evil results in evil according to the same law. . . . The law of *karma* is the law of nature, which rules the world; it is definite, unbiased, and straightforward. It wields absolute power. As such we can call it God. . . .

Christianity is more than a religion of faith. It is a religion of action, wisdom, love, and self-help.

The following Biblical passages confirm the above conclusion. In John 6:68, Simon Peter answers Jesus, saying: "You have the words of eternal life." Buddhists believe that eternal life cannot be gained simply through faith, but rather through following the way taught by Jesus Christ. Only after a person has actually experienced eternal life by practice may he be said to have perfect faith. Here "eternal life" must be understood in the language of Dhamma [truth], for its meaning escapes the comprehension of faith but is perceptible to the intellect. Although Peter was a poor fisherman, he was wise enough to see clearly that this new life was quite different from ordinary existence. After he actually realized it, he saw his previous life as a meaningless event. The knowledge gained from Peter's experience led him to the understanding of eternal life in an ultimate sense. Eternal life cannot be achieved only by faith, but must be gained by the understanding leading to the ultimate goal.

In John 6:63, Jesus says: "It is the spirit that gives life, the flesh is of no avail; the words that I have spoken to you are spirit and life." These words have no meaning or purpose if one accepts them in the terms of common language, memorizing and blindly believing them without an inquiring attitude. They are expressed in Dhamma-language, and, therefore, must be perceived by the intellect, then used as a guide to action. The full meaning of this passage is revealed only in correct and upright practice accompanied by careful attention. . . . In this context, spirit does not mean mind as is commonly supposed, and neither does life refer to life in the ordinary sense. Life here signifies the eternal life which knows no death. These words do not apply to common experience but rather to the way of Jesus which results in emancipation. This way has no place in a religion based only on faith but must be found in a religion of wisdom and action.

Faith itself need not always be blind, but may operate on the higher level of religious experience. In this sense faith implies a dedicated, disciplined mind trained by earnest practice in the hope of a higher goal. In Matt. 21:21, Jesus declares, "If you have faith and never doubt, . . . if you say to this mountain, 'Be taken up and cast into the sea,' it will be done." Jesus repeats this principle in different words in Matt. 17:20, "If you have faith as a grain of mustard seed, you will say to this mountain, 'Move from here to there,' and it will move; and nothing will be impossible to you." Matthew 14:31 depicts Jesus restraining Peter, saving him from sinking in the lake, and accusing him of insufficient faith. In these examples faith is not a passive acquiescence but a most active, highly concentrated state of mind. This type of faith required by God can never be blind. In fact, blind belief in authority without a basis of correct understanding seems to be completely absent from the teaching of Jesus Christ. How then is it possible to love others and destroy our egoism by faith alone, without knowing why we have this faith? Will such faith be powerful enough to move mountains? If one interprets the word "mountain" in the Buddhist sense, it means the selfishness which hinders us on our way to the truth. It is a mountain much heavier than ordinary mountains on the earth. Buddhists too have faith. They believe that we can move mountains in order to reach the truth. Therefore, a religion like Buddhism or Christianity should not be called a religion of faith; it should rather be described as a system of prescribed action based on the highest knowledge pertaining to the absolute truth (divine wisdom or God).

In Matt. 6:14–15, Jesus says: "For if you forgive men their trespasses, your heavenly Father also will forgive you." Here again more than simple faith is needed if a Christian wishes to attain emancipation. He must *act*, by forgiving others;

only then can he be free from his wrongs, for he receives forgiveness in turn. From the Buddhist viewpoint, this way of action illustrates the principle of self-help. If a person helps himself first, by doing good deeds, God or Karma will necessarily respond in kind and assist him. Forgiving others' wrongs signifies a desire for benefit, not merely a desire to please God. Buddhists believe that such acts actually do result in personal benefit. Furthermore, they feel that the same principle may be found in Christianity, even though centuries of varied interpretations have ended by characterizing this religion simply as a way of faith.

In Matt. 7:18–20, Jesus points out in a parable that a person is recognized as good or bad by his actions. This accords well with Buddhist teaching. In Matt. 6:33 are found these words: "Set your mind on God's kingdom and his justice before everything else, and all the rest will come to you as well" [NEB]. In a superficial sense, this statement appears to demand absolute devotion based only on faith. However, when interpreted with Buddhist reasoning, it acquires a different meaning. The expression "Set your mind on God's kingdom and his justice before everything else . . ." implies a total sacrifice, which in Pāli is *paṭinissagga*, literally, "giving up." When a person has not yet set his mind on the ultimate goal, the kingdom of God, he feels that he possesses many things which really belong to Nature or to God. In other words, he is attached to natural things by his sense of "I" or "my." If that attachment is very strong, then his feeling of self becomes so intense that it results in egoism. But if a person sets his mind on his goal, the kingdom of God, then he just returns all his possessions back to God or to Nature by harboring no attachment or feeling of ownership. In this way he gains emancipation, and an eternal peace and happiness. This process of giving up is the most desirable thing to do, for the simple reason that these things actually do not belong to us. Even our minds and our bodies are not ours; they belong to Dhamma or God. By Dhamma, God and Nature, Buddhists mean the absolute truth. The mind that is free from the feeling of self or ego is, therefore, the mind that has reached the absolute truth. This state of mind is called *lokut-tara-Dhamma,* the supermundane. In the light of this interpretation, Jesus' statement reveals itself to be a statement on the supermundane level. Turning to the kingdom of God is not mere faith; it is *karma,* the intentional action leading to the highest state, the complete cessation of suffering. When one attains this state, then there is nothing left for him to do and he is free.

Matthew 7:2 states, "And whatever measure you deal out to others will be dealt back to you" [NEB], a phrase in harmony with the Buddhist law of *karma.* But by whom will it be dealt back to you? Obviously your neighbors who exchange goods with you would not deal with you in this way. From the perspective of the language of Dhamma, the statement implies that God or the law of *karma* will give the results of your actions back to you. In Matt. 7:12 we read: "Always treat others as you would like them to treat you" [NEB]. This position also agrees with the law of *karma.* If a person wants God to love him, to fulfill his wishes, he must first love God and do what God wishes him to do. In other words, he must simply act according to the law of *karma,* equating it with God, the absolute. This principle is the one of self-help explored earlier.

Matthew 7:7 reads, "Ask, and it will be given you; seek, and you will find; knock, and it will be opened to you." The word "ask" here refers to an earnest effort; mere faith is not enough, nor is lengthy time spent in prayer. It is we who are to ask; it is we who are to seek; it is we who are to knock; and it is only when we do so that God is moved to respond. In Matt. 11:29, Jesus says: "Take my yoke upon you." He clearly declares that a Christian must persevere in action in order to gain emancipation, not merely profess his faith. . . . Matthew 12:49–50 states: "Here are my mother and my brothers! For whoever does the will of my Father in heaven is my brother, and sister, and mother." In this statement the word "does" is used rather than an expression of passive submission to external authority. Jesus emphasized practice rather than uninformed faith; rejecting the common standards of family relationships, he accepted only those who followed the will of God as his brothers, sisters, and mothers. This important principle again stresses action rather than faith. . . . Matthew 19:17 gives this instruction: "If you would enter life, keep the commandments." Here the word "keep" refers to practice with the aim of achieving the highest goal. Something more than an unknowing faith in the commandments is needed if one wishes to live an eternal life. That is practice.

Summing up, we can see that the Christian ideals of forbearance, forgiveness, helping others, and loving others as oneself agree with the Buddhist ideal of practice. The above quotations are clear proof that the Gospel of Matthew contains many points in accord with Buddhist teaching. . . . In both Christianity and Buddhism, it is not enough to have faith or a feeling of devotion without the practice of wise intentional actions. Even the simplest devotional prayer is a kind of action, since it involves one's body, speech, and mind. The phenomenon of faith also can be a wholesome mental action provided that faith is based on understanding and springs from the intention to find a sure refuge for oneself. Blind faith based only on superficial comprehension cannot be regarded as wholesome karmic action.

If we approach Christianity with a different outlook, we may discover other points of agreement with Buddhist teaching. With this aim in mind, can we consider Christianity a religion of wisdom and understanding?

In Matt. 18:7 we read: "Woe to the world for temptations to sin!" To Jesus, the world abounded in obstacles to the right way; but Christianity gives the light to point out that way. It asserts that the only competent guide in whom one should have faith is the Light of Wisdom. This light is God. To believe in God is therefore to follow the light of divine wisdom.

. . . From the Buddhist viewpoint, then, Christianity does preach wisdom as an element of faith [but not as a consequence of faith].

Matthew 13:23 says: "As for what was sown on good soil, this is he who hears the word and understands it; he indeed bears fruit, and yields, in one case a hundredfold, in another sixty, and in another thirty." Here Jesus declares "who hears the word and *understands,*" not "who hears the word and *believes.*" A Buddhist would explain this statement by saying, "Jesus wants a follower who understands the words he hears, not just believes what he hears." In Matt. 13:20–21, this interpretation becomes clearer: "As for what was sown on rocky ground, this is he who hears the word and immediately receives it with joy; yet he has no root in himself, but endures for a while, and when tribulation or persecution arises on account of the word, immediately he falls away." A person who clearly understands the teachings is firm and steadfast in his belief; but he who believes too quickly is like the seed sown in rocky ground, which dries up in the sun and bears no fruit. His belief quickly withers under stress. Here too Christianity emphasizes wisdom.

In Matt. 7:4–5, Jesus says: "Or how can you say to your brother, 'Let me take the speck out of your eye,' when there is the log in your own eye? You hypocrite, first take the log out of your own eye, and then you will see clearly to take the speck out of your brother's eye." This verse agrees with the teaching of the Enlightened One recorded in the *Dhamma-pāda:*

> One should first establish oneself in what is proper,
> Then only should one instruct another;
> Such a wise man will not be reproached.
>
> As he instructs others so should he himself act,
> Himself fully controlled, he should control others;
> For difficult, indeed, is self-control.
>
> *(Attavagga, 2–3.)*

In *Attavagga* 3 the expression "so should he himself act" obviously means "so should he himself instruct." In the light of the second verse, this phrase implies that a teacher should first be conversant in the lessons before he tries to instruct others in them. In other words, he must first clear his eyes with the light of God, with divine wisdom, before he tries to clear another's. The removal of one's own log therefore involves wisdom rather than faith alone. . . .

Another point of agreement between Christianity and Buddhism concerns the freedom of reasoned thought, a principle expounded in the *Kalama Sutta* of the Buddhist canon. In Matt. 12:12, Jesus says: "So it is lawful to do good on the sabbath." Jesus argued this point against the Pharisees, a traditional Hebrew sect who prohibited any act on the sabbath, including healing the sick. In repudiating this narrow viewpoint, Jesus taught that everything beneficial to the people could be done on this day. The Buddha too favored the spirit of free thought; he advised his followers not to adhere to merely traditional beliefs *(maparamparaya)*. While arguing with the Pharisees, Jesus declared: "I tell you, something greater than the temple is here" (Matt. 12:6). Then he added: "For the Son of man is lord of the sabbath" (Matt. 12:8). Jesus concluded through reasoned wisdom that the old traditions had been misunderstood, and he urged the Pharisees to cast away their misinterpretations. He maintained that certain acts could be performed on the sabbath, even though this day was observed as a holy day of God. Speaking in the name of God, Jesus condemned blind and hypocritical ritual action and encouraged the common people to use their intellects, to interpret the sabbath laws [for the benefit of humankind]. The Pharisees, however, were too blind to understand Jesus' words. Consequently they devised a plot to kill him. From the Buddhist viewpoint, Jesus' attitude toward free thought [i.e., thought that transcends convention] sympathizes with the Buddha's teaching and accords with a religion of wisdom.

Matthew 15:1–11 depicts a group of Pharisees and lawyers

from Jerusalem asking Jesus this question: "Why do your disciples transgress the tradition of the elders? For they do not wash their hands when they eat." He replied: "Not what goes into the mouth defiles a man, but what comes out of the mouth, this defiles a man" (Matt. 15:11). When queried by Peter, Jesus explained his meaning: "But what comes out of the mouth proceeds from the heart, and this defiles a man. For out of the heart come evil thoughts, murder, adultery, fornication, theft, false witness, slander. These are what defile a man; but to eat with unwashed hands does not defile a man" (Matt. 15:18–20). This statement reveals that Christianity, like Buddhism, is not a religion of rituals and does not emphasize outward forms and superstitious acts. Unfortunately, many rituals have in time covered the essence of Christianity so completely that they have become its fundamental meaning.

Jesus had little regard for the ordinary family relationships of father, mother, brother, and sister as they are understood in conventional language. As mentioned above, he felt that only those who conformed with the way of his heavenly Father were his near relatives. Jesus went beyond these old traditions in order to reach the highest truth. Buddhists have the same attitude toward family relationships. One is reborn in the family of the Noble Ones *(ariyāya jatiya jato)* and therefore comes to have sisters, brothers, mother, and father in a different sense. The new life characterized by these relationships is the life of wisdom, of the highest truth.

Now that we have discussed Christianity as a religion of wisdom, let us introduce several other points for further comparison. In Matt. 19:21, Jesus says: "If you would be perfect, go, sell what you possess and give to the poor . . . ; and come, follow me." To follow Jesus means to live a homeless life, without a permanent dwelling, without family, and without money. Indeed, Jesus lived in this way and encouraged his disciples to do the same so that they might not be hindered on their way to emancipation. Matthew 6:24 illustrates the importance of the homeless life: "No one can serve two masters." A person either wins riches in this world or wins the kingdom of God; he cannot have both at the same time. Again Jesus says: "Truly, I say to you, it will be hard for a rich man to enter the kingdom of heaven. Again I tell you, it is easier for a camel to go through the eye of a needle than for a rich man to enter the kingdom of God" (Matt. 19:23–24). These references affirm the Christian's highest pursuit to be a homeless life coupled with renunciation of the sense-pleasures in order to attain the state of perfection. In Pāli this ideal is known as *nekkhamma* or *nekkhamma-parami*. Jesus himself was an outstanding example of this kind of life.

One of the central elements of Buddhism is the Middle Way, a practical method [aimed at the highest realization] that avoids sensual pleasure on the one hand and self-torture or self-mortification on the other. This way may also be called the golden mean. By following it, one retains enough bodily and mental strength to perform one's duties in this world. Jesus also favored the golden mean. He himself lived according to it and urged his followers to do the same. In Matt. 11:29–30 he declares: "Take my yoke upon you, and learn from me; for I am gentle and lowly in heart, and you will find rest for your souls. For my yoke is easy, and my burden is light." By upholding the golden mean, Christianity too avoids the extremities of laxity and strictness in attitude and conduct. How similar this principle is to the Middle Way of the Buddha!

Another characteristic statement of Buddhism is: "Dhamma is to be realized by oneself" (in Pāli, *paccattāni*). In other words, "Dhamma is to be understood and realized within by turning inward" (in Pāli, *ajjhattāni*). Buddhists believe that a wise man finds "no need to accept or to refer to any authority, be it one's own teacher, or one's own scriptures, or even some trustworthy person" *(Kalama Sutta, Aṅguttara-Nikāya)*. Christian teaching agrees with this principle, for Jesus says: "As the scripture has said, 'Out of his heart shall flow rivers of living water' " (John 7:38). In other words, any person who believes in Jesus by practicing his teaching will drink the water of eternity which will flow out from within himself. The teaching implied here concurs with a Buddhist viewpoint. One must cast off the life of the world in order to enter the divine life which belongs to Nature or God. When a person has achieved this, he will taste sublime peace and inner calmness. In Buddhism, this achievement is called Nirvāna, the extinction of the suffering that previously existed within oneself. The Buddha says: "The world, the cause of the world, the cessation of the world, and the path leading to the cessation of the world—all this has been pointed out by the Tathāgata to be found and realized in this fathom-long body with perception and consciousness" *(Rohitassa Sutta, Aṅguttara-Nikāya)*. We can find everything in this worldly body, if we only know *what* and *how* to practice. God, Jesus Christ, the grace of God, the waters of eternity— all may be discovered within the individual through practice. Manifold suffering, Satan and the flames of hell also can be found in one's self, depending on one's actions. If a person practices the way leading to the highest truth, he can find the kingdom of God within himself, but his progress depends on his method and level of practice. The crucial question is whether he is ready to give up his life in the sensual world. The answer will determine the outcome of his rebirth in the kingdom of God within himself or rebirth in his inner hell. A Christian is born anew (John 3:3) or enters life (Matt. 19:17) when he is able to act in a [God-given] way here and now, in this world. The Buddhist principle that Dhamma must be realized by oneself and within oneself is as much a part of Christianity [as it is of Buddhism]. . . .

A striking similarity between the teachings of the Buddha and those of Jesus occurs in the last words spoken by them to their disciples. Jesus says: "Go therefore . . . , teaching them to observe all that I have commanded you; and lo, I am with you always, to the close of the age" (Matt. 28:19–20).

The Buddha says: "The Dhamma and the Discipline (Dhamma-Vinaya) that have been formulated and taught you will be your teacher in time to come after my passing away" *(Mahāparanibbāna Sutta, Dīgha-Nikāya)*. The Buddha concludes: "All things are subject to decay, strive with diligence." At the time of physical death, both the Buddha and Jesus Christ implored their disciples to take up their practices earnestly and firmly. They both assured their disciples of their continued presence, meaning that the Dhamma-truth personified in themselves would be perpetuated in the minds of those who practiced it. In Christianity the presence of Jesus is called "living by the spirit." For Buddhists, the same state is called "to live according to the Dhamma-Vinaya which is always in the mind, and is characterized as the purity, brightness, and abiding calm of the follower." The passage "I am with you always, to the close of the age" must be interpreted in the language of Dhamma. Given this interpretation, based on the wisdom of understanding, we can see that the Buddha and Jesus are really living with us always. . . .

When he was about to die, Jesus commanded his disciples to propagate his teaching to all nations. The Buddha, after his enlightenment in the first part of his preaching career, realized the necessity of spreading the Dhamma and pointed his first sixty disciples in sixty separate directions, telling them to preach the truth. Both Jesus and the Buddha cherished the common hope that the truth would be given to all people in the world. Jesus says: "Go therefore and make disciples of all nations, baptizing them in the name of the Father and of the Son and of the Holy Spirit" (Matt. 28:19). The Buddha uttered these words: "Go ye, O Bhikkhus, and wander forth for the gain of the many, for the welfare of the many, in compassion for the world, for the good, for the gain, for the welfare of gods and men. Proclaim, O Bhikkhus, the Doctrine glorious, preach ye a life of holiness, perfect and pure" *(Mahāvagga, Vinaya-Pitaka,* 4:39–32). As described by their founders, Christianity and Buddhism are both universal religions; they exist wherever truly religious people practice their religion in the most perfect way. If religious persons show respect for each religious founder and for the Dhamma-truth at the core of each religion, they will understand this interpretation. Devotion to one religion results in the cessation of self-interest and self-importance and therefore leads to a realization of the universality and unity of all religions. . . .

The word "God" always conveys a hidden Dhamma-[or spiritual] meaning, and may therefore be interpreted in religious language. Chapters 1 to 3 of Genesis, describing God's creation, represent for Buddhists a spiritual, Dhammic creation, not the material creation of the universe. Man evolved slowly, developing from a lower animal-like stage to the higher level considered now to be human. He developed both physically and spiritually. Strangely enough, some Christian denominations still do not accept the scientifically based theory of man's evolution from an apelike creature. This viewpoint has caused a number of problems, for the age of man given in Genesis has not been confirmed by research. According to scientific theory, man appeared physically approximately two hundred thousand years ago, and the age of the earth is not less than a billion years. Calculating from the Biblical figures, the creation must have occurred eight thousand to ten thousand years ago. Hence the world created in Genesis cannot be the material world but necessarily points to the Dhammic world of the mind. . . .

For Buddhists the religious world means the world within the mind of man, not the physical, ordinary world outside man. The Buddha says: "The world, its cause, its annihilation, the path towards its annihilation—all these are declared by the Tathāgata as being complete in this fathom-long body, inclusive of perception and mind" *(Rohitassa Sutta, Aṅguttara-Nikāya)*. . . . [God's] creation focused entirely on spiritual elements. Ignorance itself ceaselessly creates these illusions which are marked by a widespread dualism: good and evil, happiness and suffering, man and woman, and so on. Under their apparent dualism, however, the essence of natural phenomena lies hidden, invisible to ordinary perception. This essence is the *asankhata-dhamma,* the unconstituted, unformed, unconditioned nature of all things. Because of their inability to perceive the *asankhata-dhamma,* people grasp the apparent, changing shadows of things and endow them with reality; consequently they suffer.

The law of Nature is *asankhata* in that it is impersonal [and unlimited]. It acts in everything, in every atom perceptible to the senses and to the mind, and in the actions and reactions of these psychological functions as well. Through religious practice anyone may perceive the *asankhata-dhamma* hidden in everything, active in everything. To see it is to cast off illusion and see God. To see it is to live in the kingdom of God without suffering, for suffering results from clinging to the self. When the false sense of "I" dissolves, suffering too is destroyed. In Christianity, freedom from suffering is called entering into the kingdom of God. . . .

Buddhists use the word "Dhamma" in other ways as well. In textbooks, Dhamma frequently designates the collection of recorded sayings of the Buddha. Dhamma as the Buddha's teaching consists of practical aspects to be studied and followed in order to attain to realization, or to Dhamma in its religious sense. Many other meanings of the word exist, just as in Christianity the word "God" implies many different things. However, for those who practice Buddhism and perceive the highest truth, all the meanings of Dhamma converge in one essential core.

Having examined the meaning of the word "God" in religious language, we must also discuss the God of conventional terminology to discern the problems stemming from these two meanings.

The word "God" in its ordinary sense has caused many serious problems in interpretation. If the word is interpreted incorrectly, or is not interpreted at all, it cannot complement the ideas of other fields of knowledge. Instead, it requires blind faith. Often people relinquish their own religion and embrace a new one, or abandon religion altogether, simply because of false interpretations. These misunderstandings also create friction among religious groups.

Suppose we tell a child that God is omnipresent, and the child responds, "Even in a dog?" How then shall we answer? The child only recognizes the word "God" in its conventional context; he cannot understand how God could exist in such things. But it is impossible to say that God is not in these things, for if God is not everywhere, then he is not God. The God of ordinary language denotes a personal being with human emotions, like anger and love. He cannot exist in a dog, for it is too earthy, too unpleasant, too lowly for the presence of the highest. However, the God of religious language, called Dhamma, is without emotions, impersonal, beyond cleanliness and dirtiness. Therefore this God can be in everything, even in a dog.

Some Buddhist sects employ other terms to characterize Dhamma, such as *buddhabhava* (Buddha-nature), *suññatā* (voidness or emptiness), and *tathatā* (suchness). Because these terms do not have a personal referent, they apply to all things. The word "Buddha-nature" denotes the absence of self in a person called Buddha. This Buddha-nature is Dhamma, which here implies the understanding of the voidness of self seen at various stages of development. The growth of this understanding resembles the germination and development of a seed, culminating in a fully matured tree. Like an ungerminated seed, Buddha-nature may lie dormant in a person's consciousness; it may sprout and become fully grown as in the man who has attained enlightenment. Each stage of this development can be called Buddha-nature. Furthermore, each stage contains in an equal measure the characteristic of voidness, but it is hidden deep and is unseen on the surface. The Buddha says, "He who sees the Dhamma sees me" *(Itivuttaka, Khuddaka-Nikāya)*. He who sees only the person of the Buddha has not really seen him. Only when a person sees the true Dhamma in the Buddha's body, in his own body, and in everything, does he see the Buddha. When he sees only the body of the Buddha, he sees according to the common meaning of the word "see"; but when he sees the Dhamma, he sees in the different, religious sense of the word. He has then seen the true Buddha. Naturally the Buddha as he is understood in conventional language cannot possibly be in all places at all times. But the Buddha of religious language can. In the same way, God in ordinary terms is simply a word to be used when speaking to children or to the intellectually immature. But God as Dhamma is everywhere, acting in all things. . . . Everything material, even the smallest stone, has a spiritual dimension.

The story of creation found in Genesis refers to the creation of the human spirit. . . . Adam and Eve, before they took the forbidden fruit from the tree of knowledge, revealed man's prior inability to distinguish between good and evil, male and female, clothed and naked, husband and wife. Even in the act of sexual intercourse male and female were ignorant of their sexual roles. After eating the fruit of the knowledge of good and evil, man became proud of his separateness, and his knowledge of the difference between good and evil. His discriminating mind, however, led him to ethical conflicts and a kind of suffering unknown to other animals. Because man ate of the fruit of knowledge, he is burdened with birth, growth, decay, and death; but if he had eaten the fruit of the tree of life, he would have gained an everlasting life, as everlasting as God himself. Life here means not-dying, for life is that which is eternal. The moment man tastes the fruit of life he will live; he will secure the wisdom known in Buddhism as *amata-Dhamma,* the Deathless State, the seeing of Not-self. In this state there is no self to be born, to grow old, to die. In Buddhism, a person who has attained Arahantship is said to have gained the deathless, or entered the immortal city; he consciously discovers Nirvāna within this very lifetime, as an individual. The Genesis account, therefore, points to what we call in Buddhism *amata-Dhamma* or *lokuttara-Dhamma* [eternal or transcendental truth]. Like the word "life" the terms "God," "the world," and "the tree of the knowledge of good and evil" can all be given a Dhamma-sense [or higher meaning]. Indeed this sort of rendering is necessary if a person is to understand these words properly. He will then find that Christianity, as well as Buddhism and many other religions, embodies a profound truth on a supermundane level. The creation story in Genesis therefore reflects more than an ancient Hebrew myth as some have called it.

Dhamma-language can also be applied in the following examples. Genesis 1:26 reads: "Then God said, 'Let us make man in our image, after our likeness.'" These words have caused much confusion. Some scholarly Christian works have asserted, with good reason, that God is formless. However, many people do not believe this, since the Bible clearly states that God created man with a form similar to his own. This literal viewpoint has resulted from a false interpretation of the text. When the Bible says that man was created after God's likeness, it means that man is capable of the power of God, that he can unite with God; if man partakes of the tree of life, he will indeed become [like] God. God has merely postponed man's chance for the time being by directing man away from the life-giving tree (Gen. 3:24). To discuss God as if he were endowed with a bodily form is senseless.

In Gen. 2:7, we read: "Then the LORD God formed man of dust from the ground, and breathed into his nostrils the breath of life; and man became a living being." The man formed of dust here refers to the man of the remote past, a physical body without intelligent consciousness, a dumb animal in human form. As time passed, this manlike creature began to distinguish himself from all the other animals; God then was said to breathe into him the breath of life. God's act can be understood as a new creation, the creation of the spirit or the mind, distinctive in man. The creation of the world in Genesis is therefore identical with the creation of the spirit.

Genesis 2:21–22 states: "So the LORD God caused a deep sleep to fall upon the man, and while he slept took one of his ribs and closed up its place with flesh; and the rib which the LORD God had taken from the man he made into a woman and brought her to the man."

How can one accept this passage as it stands, without searching for its concealed meaning? From the Buddhist viewpoint, it is understood to declare the essential difference between the rights and functions of men and women. Another statement in Gen. 6:2 supports this inference; there, man is called "son of God" and woman "daughter of man." Man was created from the earth, a symbol of strength; woman, a part of man, was merely created from man's body. Whereas man is called the "son of God," woman is merely the "daughter of man." How can the two be equal in their rights and functions? Indeed, God did not intend man and woman to possess the same likeness or potentiality, for a woman bears children and must feed them from her breast, while a man cannot. The modern attempt to place both sexes in the same occupation conflicts with God's intentions and furthermore opposes nature. If a woman wants to be a man, then she must undergo an operation. This procedure would be far better than her continual deception of others, the outward show she stages in contradiction of her inner nature. In addition, it would not controvert the will of God.

Like Christianity, Buddhism too has not attributed to women the same rights and functions as men. The Buddha said: "It is not possible for a woman to become a Buddha but it is quite possible for a man to become so" *(Attanapali, Ekakanipata, Anguttara-Nikāya)*. Other sayings declare it inappropriate for a woman to become an empress or a Brahma. In the *Catukka-Nipāta, Anguttara-Nikāya,* the Lord Buddha approves the customs observed by Indian women of the time, which forbade them to sit in parliament, engage in highly specialized work, or travel in the country of Kamboja. The last restriction may be compared with today's custom of going abroad for study. The reasons for these prohibitions are also given; in general it is thought that women lack the physical stamina and the willpower to do these things. Nature has created woman with a different objective. Should she replace man in his role, she would not fulfill her duty on earth, and many new problems would arise. . . . We may conclude that the Biblical narrative is quite correct in its treatment of men and women. . . . It is not a mere absurdity, nor an ancient Hebrew myth.

In Gen. 2:16–17 we find: "And the LORD God commanded the man, saying, 'You may freely eat of every tree of the garden; but of the tree of the knowledge of good and evil you shall not eat, for in the day that you eat of it you shall die.' " If this text is taken blindly in its literal sense, it is very awkward. Why would God have spoken these words? God created man and loved him dearly. Why then should God forbid man to gain knowledge? We must first unearth the ordinary meaning of the passage, conveyed in conventional language, before we can comprehend its real meaning. The following explanation may simplify our task. A person's suffering results from his attachment to what he considers good and evil. At times, he is so plagued by the hatred of evil that he dare not act at all; other times he is so overwrought with thoughts of doing good that he cannot sleep at night. Some people even commit suicide to escape the results of their actions. Such attachment to good and evil generates desire, craving, and illusion, which are themselves suffering. Moreover, out of attachment grow greed, anger, and delusion, which are causes of suffering. But as soon as man sheds his clinging to good and evil, and releases himself from the idea of virtue and sin to live entirely beyond these conceptions, he is said to have attained . . . the state of Nirvāna. When God forbade man to know good and evil, he did so not out of a merciless desire to leave man a mere beast, but rather out of kindness. He wanted to keep man away from contact with the root cause of suffering, to preserve him from a spiritual death. For this reason God said, "for in the day that you eat of it you shall die." Whenever a person conceives of good and evil, and attaches himself to them, he immediately encounters a new form of suffering. This suffering, worse than any other, is a spiritual death.

Here another riddle presents itself for solution. Although it is quite correct to consider the eating of the forbidden fruit man's original sin, since at that time he first fell into the abyss of dualism which has plagued him for countless generations, some people may not feel that the actual sin of the first man has been passed on to posterity; rather, that sin applies only to the individual. In fact, man in the past was imperfect, and the same imperfection, the same continual delusion, torments us now. If we interpret the text in this way, original sin in Christianity is easily understood. Furthermore, Buddhists would concur with this interpretation, identifying it with the Noble Truth of Buddhism which urges people to hold no attachment to good or evil, for attachment inevitably brings suffering.

The tree of life, whose fruit could render man immortal, does not literally figure in any subsequent Biblical passage. Yet, in a way, it occurs in the words of Christ. He often spoke of the path toward eternal life, which may be compared with taking fruit of the tree of life. Indeed, Christ extended the opportunity to partake of that fruit to Adam's entire progeny. Buddhism cannot offer an analogy here, but it too has concentrated on the observation of principles aimed at eliminating attachments. When a person has tasted the fruit of the tree of life he is said to have attained the *amata-Dhamma,* the state of immortality above all concerns with death. In this state, there is no one to be born and no one to die. There exists only one infinite state—Dhamma or God— forever clear in one's consciousness. This is the forbidden fruit understood in Dhamma-terms, common to both Buddhism and Christianity.

Our last example is Gen. 6:5–7: "The LORD saw that the

wickedness of man was great in the earth, and that every imagination of the thoughts of his heart was only evil continually. And the LORD was sorry that he had made man on the earth, and it grieved him to his heart. So the LORD said, 'I will blot out man whom I have created from the face of the ground, man and beast and creeping things and birds of the air, for I am sorry that I have made them.' "

If this passage is understood in the Dhamma-sense, it becomes clear that God can make a mistake, for everything is in God, including wisdom and ignorance. Because God is all-powerful he must contain in himself the power to err. Furthermore, any creation is an act of ignorance, while non-creation is wisdom. When God states that he will destroy even the creeping things and the birds of the air, which are completely innocent of any wrongdoing, he reveals his remorse for creating the world. He realizes that any act of creation is to be pitied and abhorred, for creation is suffering. To refrain from creating is to achieve calmness of mind. The dissolution of the desire to create is the annihilation of the growth of the self. The person who aspires to such dissolution will come to detest the cycles of rebirth, or the wheels of becoming, known as *vatta-saṁsāra*.

Although the Bible literally states that God intended to destroy the world, he never actually did. Destruction, here, must be understood in its Dhamma-meaning. (In the same way Adam did not immediately die when he tasted the forbidden fruit.) The phrase "destruction of the world" figuratively represents man's true realization of the misery born from his desire to create. Yet in spite of God's threat, people still habitually crave things and cannot restrain themselves. Consequently they must bear the miseries of their [predecessors]. The loathing of the desire to create may be likened to the dawn of *lokuttara-Dhamma,* the supermundane, in the mind of man, gradually leading to his future realization. The sublime feeling of realization is God acting in the form of human wisdom; for Buddhists it is Nirvāna, a state of non-becoming achieved through Dhamma-principles.

In his very essence, the true God is above right and wrong, good and evil, although these concepts are fully contained in him. The terms "good and evil," "right and wrong," are ideas formed by men and, therefore, neither attributable to God nor meaningful in his context. Pestilence and a peaceful life are identical in God's sight and must be treated as a single entity. For this reason, natural calamities such as floods, fires, and plagues signify God's will just as their absence does; life and death too are equally the will of God. There is no difference between them for him. But for human beings, good and evil are quite different; men prefer the one and spurn its contrary. Those who have truly absorbed themselves in God or Dhamma will not see good and evil as opposites, but will treat both as equally meaningless. Nor will they dislike one or the other.

In the same way, to call God pleased or angry is to speak in conventional language . . . but when one grasps the higher meaning he begins to feel close to God, to worship him with unfailing love until he admits the ultimate supremacy of God. Then he realizes that nothing is higher than God, and that God is [merely] known by different names: Dhamma in Buddhism or the Tao in Taoism among others.

Whatever can be said of God in conventional language, therefore, can always be rendered into Dhamma-language. When people have perfectly grasped the Dhamma-meaning, they will derive great benefit from it. God is the sum total and the outlet of all things worldly and unworldly. As such he may be called the Father and the Primary Cause. He simultaneously creates and destroys the world, for world denotes both the spiritual world and the world of delusion within the human mind. . . .

## A CHRISTIAN RESPONSE
## TO BUDDHADĀSA

The lengthy selections from Bhikkhu Buddhadāsa's lectures on Buddhism and Christianity serve to illustrate the main thrust of this volume, namely, that interreligious dialogue is an encounter of religious persons rather than religious systems. Buddhadāsa's understanding of Theravāda Buddhism does not fit neatly into textbook categories. Hence, if we approach his interpretation of Buddhism from a textbook perspective, we run the risk of sidetracking the dialogical enterprise by trying to decide how Buddhadāsa compares with some manual or other that systematically sets forth the philosophy of Theravāda. Such a comparison may be interesting in its own right but, at least in the beginning stages, it jeopardizes the validity of dialogue. Our obligation is to try to understand Buddhadāsa's "faith," the way in which he has appropriated and interpreted Buddhism. Dialogue begins when we enter into such an understanding, rather than some static abstraction which, in Buddhadāsa's view, does not represent the truth anyway. The truth cannot finally be captured in neat categories to be filed away and forgotten. The truth continually challenges us where we actually are, cutting through the distortions of where we imagine we have been, and vainly hope we might go.

With this existentialist orientation Buddhadāsa has a healthy dose of impatience with historical knowledge. His distinction between Old and New Testaments reflects this impatience. Of what ultimate value are the myths and histories of the Hebrew scriptures? he asks. They may help us understand the background for the teachings of Jesus, but they are as likely to so preoccupy the scholar that he will lose his soul in the process. Even a study of the New Testament runs this danger: "The few pages devoted to the Sermon on the Mount in the Gospel of Matthew embody all the practical means for attaining freedom from suffering." The Sermon on the Mount is not the only part of Matthew that Buddhadāsa finds appealing. Matthew and John are his principal New Testament sources. While this selection might stem from the nature of his study, the personalistic and mystical side of John's and Matthew's preoccupation with discipline and structure ties in well with Buddhadāsa's approach to religion. His interpretation of faith leans heavily on Matthew as he seeks to show that Christianity does not, in fact, intend faith as a blind giving up of self-effort.

Buddhadāsa's primary concern, of course, is that religious people not confuse the wheat with the chaff as they go about the practice of living. Be about the main task of saving your soul, obeying the will of God, reaching for the truth: "Many Christian leaders preach their religion without mentioning the essential meaning of Christianity. Buddhist monks, too, often expound only the outward forms of Buddhism, without grasping the essence of Dhamma." Buddhadāsa rightly criticizes all of us—Christian, Buddhist, Muslim, Hindu. The scholar can more easily get caught up in questions of historical criticism and the churchman in the issues of yet another committee meeting, then in our reason for being, in Buddhadāsa's terms, "how to eliminate the craving that gives rise to I-ness and my-ness and establish purity of mind." Dialogue with Buddhadāsa brings about a self-confrontation from which we cannot escape. How Christian is your Christianity? How Buddhist is your Buddhism? At its best, interreligious dialogue operates on this deep and profoundly personal level. It catches us up short—asking—no, demanding—self-scrutiny, integrity, and utter honesty. At some point genuine dialogue brings a judgment to bear on our own faithfulness.

Interreligious dialogue at its deepest level communicates not discursively but with a shout of agreement, a look of embarrassment, a searching moment of silence. In short, dialogue with Buddhadāsa touches us at the deepest level of our being. But dialogue must be more than moments of silent insight (otherwise people would not write books like this!). Dialogue moves on different levels—some more mundane than others. Buddhadāsa recognizes this fact in his discussion of the two levels of language. There is the "truth" (Dhamma) level to which we have been referring, and also the ordinary or conventional level. No religious system can be merely one or the other; nor, for that matter, can interreligious dialogue. Buddhadāsa's own discussion of Buddhism and Christianity obviously moves between the two. His claims about both traditions must be understood in this light. That is, religious language, whether Christian or Buddhist, has an essential (i.e., Dhamma) referent and a conventional referent. For Buddhadāsa the Dhamma referent is fundamentally the transformation of one's being, the elimination of attachment to "I" and "my." The conventional referent is the ordinary interpretation of any term determined more or less by its particular context.

To illustrate Buddhadāsa's approach, let us examine his discussion of faith. Upon reading his interpretation of faith you may have reacted critically, thinking that Buddhadāsa missed the fundamental point of this concept, namely, that faith in God's forgiveness is not contingent in the same way that the operation of *karma* is contingent upon one's actions. Buddhadāsa's understanding of the meaning of faith can be justifiably criticized, but to dismiss him on these grounds would be unfair. His interpretation of faith must be taken in part as an attack on the conventional understanding of this term, where faith means having a blind reliance on outside authority. Buddhadāsa's insistence on a more comprehensive signification of faith has much to commend it. Even if we would not agree with his characterization of faith as "a dedicated, disciplined mind trained by earnest practice in the hope of a higher goal," its variance from customary ways of conceiving faith provokes new thought on this crucial subject. Similarly, his description of both Buddhism and Christianity as systems "of prescribed action based on the highest knowledge pertaining to the absolute truth" raises the question of the relationship between faith and religious disciplines, a problem addressed in Chapter 5.

Two points in particular are worth noting about Buddhadāsa's interpretation of faith: (1) in moving between two levels of language he relates conventional or traditional expressions to a more generalized mode of expression; (2) he reverses the way most Westerners customarily think about Christianity and Buddhism on the issue of quietism. Regarding the first, Buddhadāsa clearly believes that all historical religious systems at best only approximate the truth but do not embody it. Hence, the vocabulary of any particular tradition within the context of dialogue needs to be interpreted in order to uncover its essential meaning. In regard to the second, Western Christians ordinarily think of Buddhism as world-renouncing and quietistic, and their own tradition as world-affirming and activistic. Buddhadāsa's discussion provides a corrective to such easy labels. Indeed, given the badly informed assumptions most Westerners have of Buddhism, it might strike us as incongruous that a Buddhist would so defend Christianity: "We can see that Christian ideals of forbearance, forgiveness, helping others, and loving others as oneself agree with the Buddhist ideal of practice."

Buddhadāsa's discussion of God also focuses on the distinction between levels of language and meaning. This applies to the interpretation of God as person and to the creation story. Buddhadāsa's principal criticism of the conventional understanding of God is that it depicts him in anthropomorphic terms. How can God be omnipotent and omnipresent if he is seen as "a personal being with human emotions, like anger and love"? While the Christian may have problems with Buddhadāsa's ready identification of the ultimate signification of God and Buddha-nature, his discussion raises two important questions. First, do we anthropomorphize God when we conceive of him as person (basically, what do we really intend or mean when we claim that God is person)? If so, then we create the sorts of problems Buddhadāsa suggests with his story of the child who cannot conceive how God's omnipresence could embrace a dog. Did this example startle you? Indeed, I expect that it did. Buddhadāsa's example provokes a quizzical response on our part perhaps similar to the Buddhist's response to the enigmatic *koan* of the famous Zen collection known as the *Mumonkan* which asks, Does the dog have a Buddha-nature?

A second challenge Buddhadāsa raises is whether our theology (God-talk) tends to become theology for theology's sake, thereby losing the focus on the God-person relationship. Surely God does not need us to describe and define him! From a spiritual point of view the task of theology should be to clarify for our own edification the nature of our relationship to God as the ground of our being. In Buddhadāsa's view theology is meaningless outside of religious practice aimed at discovering the truth about the nature of our existence. It is from this perspective that he claims: "To see it [the truth] is to cast off illusion and see God. To see it is to live in the kingdom of God without suffering *(dukkah)*, for suffering results from clinging to the self. When the false sense of 'I' dissolves, suffering too is destroyed. In Christianity, freedom from suffering is called entering into the kingdom of God."

Buddhadāsa's interpretation of the creation story points in another direction. Here he insists that religious language has both a spiritual or supermundane reference and an ordinary or mundane reference. From this perspective he can be incredulous that some Christians insist on a Biblical-literalistic calculation of the age of the universe and miss the fundamental meaning of the creation story. But he can also argue that the story of the priority of Adam's creation over Eve should be interpreted in commonsense terms of biological and sociological differences between men and women. Of greatest interest, perhaps, is Buddhadāsa's treatment of God's prohibition against Adam and Eve's eating of the fruit of the tree of knowledge: "When God forbade man to know good and evil, he did so not out of a merciless desire to keep man a mere beast, but rather out of kindness. He wanted to keep man away from contact with the root cause of suffering, to preserve him from a spiritual death. . . . Whenever a person conceives of good and evil, and attaches himself to them, he immediately encounters a new form of suffering. This suffering, worse than any other, is a spiritual death."

Buddhadāsa has presented a sympathetic interpretation of Christianity from a Buddhist perspective. How do we respond to it? One response would be to challenge him at those points where he is most at variance with orthodox doctrine. At best, to begin in this manner would be to keep our dialogue on a highly intellectual level. At worst, the encounter would degenerate into a series of arguments. A different approach is the one we have taken, to find in what a Buddhist has to say about Christianity a provocative challenge to our own faith. Such an approach to interreligious dialogue means neither that we must agree with the interpretation of the other person, nor that we can be sympathetic only if we hold the position that differences among religious traditions are only culturally relative. It does mean that we believe the great historic religions speak to universal human problems from which even modern, technological man is not immune, and that as Christians our own formulations of these problems and their answers have not received their final definition. Surely the Christian's faith in God's identification with the ongoing processes of history justifies us in making this claim! As Christians we are always in the process of working out our own salvation with fear and trembling. Along the way let us hope that we will meet a Buddhadāsa who can help illumine our faith to keep us from falling into "a spiritual death."

# Notes

## Chapter 1

### Approaches to Interreligious Dialogue

1. This section is indebted to E. C. Dewick, *The Christian Attitude to Other Religions* (Cambridge: The University Press, 1953).

2. Dewick, *The Christian Attitude*, p. 92

3. Helmer Ringgren, *Israelite Religion* (London: S.P.C.K., 1966), p. 47.

4. Dewick, *The Christian Attitude*, p. 103.

5. *Ibid.*, p. 105.

6. *Ibid.*, p. 106.

7. *Ibid.*, pp. 107–127.

8. *Ibid.*, p. 129.

9. *Ibid.*, p. 130.

10. F. S. C. Northrop, "Present Context and Character of the World's Religions," *The Graduate Journal,* University of Texas, Vol. VII, 1966 Supplement, p. 47.

11. For a brief historical treatment of the missionary debate on Christian approaches to non-Christian religions from the World Missionary Conference at Tambaram in 1938 to the World Council of Churches meeting in Uppsala in 1968, see Carl F. Hallencreutz, *New Approaches to Men of Other Faiths* (Geneva: World Council of Churches, 1970).

12. Hendrik Kraemer, *The Christian Message in a Non-Christian World,* 3d ed. (Kregel Publications, 1956), p. 302.

13. Hendrik Kraemer, *Religion and the Christian Faith* (The Westminster Press, 1957), pp. 45–46.

14. Kraemer, *The Christian Message,* p. 145.

15. Hendrik Kraemer, *World Religions and World Cultures* (The Westminster Press, 1960), p. 356.

16. R. C. Zaehner, *Christianity and Other Religions* (Hawthorn Books, Inc., 1964), p. 8.

17. *Ibid.*, p. 40.

18. *Ibid.*, p. 38. Italics mine.

19. R. C. Zaehner, *The Comparison of Religions* (Beacon Press, Inc., 1962), p. 180.

20. William E. Hocking, *Living Religions and a World Faith* (The Macmillan Company, 1940), p. 26.

21. *Ibid.*

22. *Ibid.*, p. 35.

23. *Ibid.*, p. 43.

24. *Ibid.*, p. 63.

25. *Ibid.*, p. 198.

26. *Ibid.*, p. 200.

27. *Ibid.*, p. 249.

28. William E. Hocking, *The Coming World Civilization* (Harper & Brothers, 1956), p. 136.

29. *Ibid.*, p. 85.

30. Klaus Klostermaier, "Dialogue—The Words of God," in Herbert Jai Singh (ed.), *Inter-Religious Dialogue* (Bangalore: The Christian Institute for the Study of Religion and Society, 1967), p. 119.

31. Klaus Klostermaier, "Hindu-Christian Dialogue," in Stanley J. Samartha (ed.), *Dialogue Between Men of Living Faiths* (Geneva: World Council of Churches, 1971), p. 20.

32. Wilfred Cantwell Smith, *The Meaning and End of Religion* (The Macmillan Company, 1962), pp. 154–155.

33. *Ibid.*, p. 156.

34. *Ibid.* Faith has a wide range of meanings—from trust in God or in Christ through fidelity to right belief. In this study there are three principal interpretations: Smith seems to use the term to mean something close to religious experience; the Pauline use of faith, which I have interpreted ontologically in terms of the New Creation; and the use of faith by Bhikkhu Buddhadāsa which correlates with the disciplined practice in hope of a higher goal.

35. *Ibid.*

36. Wilfred Cantwell Smith, "Mankind's Religiously Divided History Approaches Self-consciousness," *The Harvard Divinity Bulletin,* 29 (October 1964), p. 12.

37. Smith, *The Meaning and End of Religion,* p. 141.

38. *Ibid.,* p. 135.

39. *Ibid.,* p. 128.

40. Joachim Wach, *The Comparative Study of Religions* (Columbia University Press, 1961), pp. 30ff.

41. Smith, *The Meaning and End of Religion,* pp. 170–185.

42. *Ibid.,* p. 183. Italics mine.

43. *Ibid.,* p. 129.

44. Smith, "Mankind's Religiously Divided History," p. 8.

45. Wilfred Cantwell Smith, *The Faith of Other Men* (The New American Library of World Literature, Inc., 1963), p. 76.

46. Ninian Smart, *A Dialogue of Religions* (London: SCM Press, Ltd., 1960), p. 9.

47. Wilfred Cantwell Smith, *Questions of Religious Truth* (Charles Scribner's Sons, 1967), p. 69.

48. *Ibid.,* p. 68. Italics mine.

49. John Hick, "The Outcome: Dialogue Into Truth," in John Hick (ed.), *Truth and Dialogue in World Religions: Conflicting Truth-Claims* (The Westminster Press, 1974), pp. 145–146.

50. Smith, *Questions of Religious Truth,* p. 70.


## Chapter 2


### *In the World But Not of It*

1. Amos Wilder, *Eschatology and Ethics in the Teaching of Jesus,* rev. ed. (Harper & Brothers, 1950), p. 179.

2. *Ibid.,* p. 195.

3. *Ibid.,* p. 238.

4. Victor P. Furnish, *Theology and Ethics in Paul* (Abingdon Press, 1968), p. 210.

5. *Ibid.,* pp. 217–218.

6. A. C. McGiffert, *A History of Christian Thought,* Vol. 1 (Charles Scribner's Sons, 1953), p. 37.

7. Søren Kierkegaard, *Attack on Christendom,* tr. by Walter Lowrie (Princeton University Press, 1946), p. 181.

8. Peter Berger, *The Sacred Canopy* (Doubleday & Company, Inc., Anchor Book, 1969), p. 51.

9. Gustavo Gutiérrez, *A Theology of Liberation,* ed. and tr. by Caridad Inda and John Eagleson (Orbis Books, 1973).

10. Henry Clarke Warren, *Buddhism in Translations* (Harvard University Press, 1896), p. 352.

11. Albert C. Outler (tr. and ed.), *Augustine: Confessions and Enchiridion,* The Library of Christian Classics, Vol. VII (The Westminster Press, 1955), p. 147.

12. *Ibid.*

## Chapter 3

### *It Is No Longer I Who Live*

1. William F. Arndt and F. Wilbur Gingrich, *A Greek-English Lexicon of the New Testament and Other Early Christian Literature* (The University of Chicago Press, 1957), *"sarx,"* par. 7, p. 751.

2. Warren, *Buddhism in Translations,* pp. 131f.

3. E. A. Burtt (ed.), *The Teachings of the Compassionate Buddha* (The New American Library of World Literature, Inc., 1955), pp. 34–35.

4. Note the difference between Paul's use of faith and that of Wilfred Cantwell Smith (see Chapter 1), who interprets the concept more in terms of personal religious experience. Smith will soon publish a major study of the concepts of faith and belief which promises to be as provocative and controversial as *The Meaning and End of Religion.*

5. Raymond Bernard Blakney (ed.), *Meister Eckhart: A Modern Translation* (Harper & Row, Publishers, Inc., Harper Torchbook, 1970), p. 85.

## Chapter 4

### *True Righteousness*

1. Aurelius Augustine, "On Grace and Free Will," in Wayne A. Meeks (ed.), *The Writings of St. Paul* (W. W. Norton & Company, Inc., 1972), pp. 220–221.

2. Martin Luther, *Three Treatises,* intro. and tr. by C. M. Jacobs, A. T. W. Steinhauser, and W. A. Lambert (Muhlenberg Press, 1947), p. 265.

3. Warren, *Buddhism in Translations,* p. 214.

4. *Ibid.,* p. 216.

5. See Nārada Thera (tr.), *Dhammapāda* (Vajirarama: Colombo, 1963), pp. 1–6. Numerous other translations are available. See E. A. Burtt (ed.), *The Teachings of the Compassionate Buddha,* or Clarence H. Hamilton, *Buddhism: A Religion of Infinite Compassion.*

6. See Winston L. King, *In the Hope of Nibbāna: An Essay on Theravāda Buddhist Ethics* (The Open Court Publishing Company, 1964), Part I, for a discussion of Theravāda ethics in relationship to *karma* and Nirvāna.

## Chapter 5

### *Freedom Now!*

1. Luther, *Three Treatises,* p. 252.

2. Burtt (ed.), *The Teachings of the Compassionate Buddha,* p. 112.

3. For example, see Charles T. Tart, *Altered States of Consciousness* (Doubleday & Company, Inc., Anchor Book, 1972).

4. Lesslie Newbigin, *The Household of God* (Friendship Press, 1954), p. 51.

5. Thomas Merton, *The Wisdom of the Desert* (New Directions, 1970), p. 5.

6. Jean Leclercq, *The Love of Learning and the Desire for God,* tr. by Catharine Misrahi (The New American Library of World Literature, Inc., 1962), p. 25.

7. See Enomiya Lassalle, *Zen Meditation for Christians,* tr. by John C. Maraldo (The Open Court Publishing Company, 1974).

8. Thomas Merton, *Mystics and Zen Masters* (Dell Publishing Company, Inc., 1967), p. 209.

9. *Ibid.,* p. 203.

10. *Ibid.,* p. 204.

11. Thomas P. McDonnell (ed.), *A Thomas Merton Reader,* rev. ed. (Doubleday & Company, Inc., Image Book, 1974), p. 439.

12. Paul Reps (comp.), *Zen Flesh, Zen Bones* (Charles E. Tuttle Co., 1957), pp. 143–144.

13. William Johnston, *Christian Zen* (Harper & Row Publishers, Inc., 1971), Ch. 7.

14. *Ibid.,* pp. 64–65.


## Chapter 6

### *A Kingdom of Priests and a Holy Nation*

1. See *Christianity and Crisis,* Vol. 36, Nos. 2 and 12, for the full texts and comments on the Boston and Hartford statements.

2. Warren, *Buddhism in Translations,* Ch. V, for extensive textual references characterizing the *bhikkhu sangha.*

3. Julio R. Sabanes, "Biblical Understanding of Community," in Egbert de Vries (ed.), *Man in Community* (Association Press, 1966), p. 168.

4. McDonnell, *A Thomas Merton Reader,* pp. 182–183.


## Chapter 7

### *A Buddhist View of Christianity*

1. See Donald K. Swearer (ed.), *Toward the Truth,* by Buddhadāsa (The Westminster Press, 1971). Also Donald K. Swearer, "Thai Buddhism: Two Responses to Modernity," in E. L. Smith (ed.), *Tradition and Change in Theravada Buddhism,* Contributions to Asian Studies, Vol. 4 (Leiden: E. J. Brill, 1973), pp. 78–93.